The Child's Part

The Child's Part

edited by
PETER BROOKS

BEACON PRESS   BOSTON

Copyright © 1969 by Yale French Studies
Library of Congress Catalog card number: 78–181067
International Standard Book Number: 0–8070–6401–7
First published as a Beacon Paperback in 1972 by arrangement with Yale French Studies
Published simultaneously in Canada by Saunders of Toronto, Ltd.
Beacon Press books are published under the auspices of the Unitarian Universalist Association
All rights reserved
Printed in the United States of America
The essays in this book appeared originally in issue Number 43 of *Yale French Studies*

First published as a Beacon Paperback in 1972

Contents

3 Foreword

LIMINARY
5 Toward supreme fictions
Peter Brooks

15 At the point of origin
Philippe Ariès

THE TALE
24 From tales of warning to formulettes
Marc Soriano

44 The Grimm Brothers
Marthe Robert

THE GOLDEN AGE
57 Children's literature and bourgeois society since 1860
Isabelle Jan

73 Hetzel and the Bibliothèque d'Éducation et de Récréation
Esther S. Kanipe

85 One hundred years of illustrations in French children's books
Marion Durand

THE MASTER
97 The twilight zone: imagination and reality in Jules Verne's *Strange Journeys*
André Winandy

111 Jules Verne's image of the United States
Jean Chesneaux

THE COUNTER-MASTER	128	The language of nonsense in *Alice* *Jacqueline Flescher*
	145	What is a Boojum? *Michael Holquist*
DISSENT	165	Childhood amnesia *Richard Howard*
	171	Contributors

ILLUSTRATIONS

Cover Original drawing by Laurent de Brunhoff

29 Eighteenth-century woodcut for Perrault's *Contes*

51 Gustave Doré for *Le Petit Poucet*

87 Lorentz Froelich for *Mademoiselle Lili aux Champs-Elysées*

89 L. Bennett for *Autour du monde en quatre-vingt jours*

91 Castelli for *Jean qui grogne, Jean qui rit*

107 A. de Neuville for *Vingt mille lieues sous les mers*

Foreword

Why should we study children's literature? For those of us who have made a profession of cultural alienation — studying another people's literature — one answer is evident: to paraphrase Paul Hazard, men can truly understand one another only when they have learned the same nursery rhymes. More generally, the child's part is a vast and rich subspecies of literature, attention to which can illuminate culture, society, and literature itself. To this end, we have tried to assemble here as many diverse and divergent approaches to the subject as possible. We have necessarily fixed our focus on France — though not exclusively: the literature of reference, English, comes in more than once, it indeed can't be excluded because it is probably the richest of any in imaginative creations for children, and it helps to define the limits of the field. We are sensible to the lacunae that exist: for instance, we would have liked to have an experimental psychologist talk about how a child *reads* the books that are given to him. To a degree, the lacunae result from the situation of the child's part, its underground status in serious intellectual study. There are few "specialists" in the field, and much of this issue is the work of amateurs, which is possibly a good thing.

I want to take this occasion to express my thanks to Mlle Isabelle Jan and to Mme Marie-Claude de Brunhoff for their generous aid in preparing this issue. Acknowledgment is made to the Livre de Poche for permission to reprint two illustrations from the works of Jules Verne; and to Librairie Hachette for permission to reprint illustrations from works by the Comtesse de Ségur and P.-J. Hetzel.

P. B.

Peter Brooks

Toward supreme fictions

If we begin by asking what we mean by "children's literature," the indefinition and ambiguity of our subject is immediately apparent. We probably don't mean literature written by children, though this would be a rich field for investigation (as, for instance, in the case of the Brontë children). But do we mean literature read by children, or literature written for children? The two are not coterminous. Contributors to this issue tend to confront this primary ambiguity in two different ways: by confining their attention to literature written specifically for children (hence to a tradition of didactic origin), or by conceiving their subject as that literature which the adult world — for which it may have been written — has assigned to children (most notably, the domain of the folk tale).

Both definitions of course exclude a vast body of "children's literature," in the sense of works read during childhood: books written for adults but somehow appropriated by children. From the chivalric novels which nourished Montaigne as well as Don Quixote, through the adventure tales sold in little blue-covered volumes by peddlers, through the *Arabian Nights* to *The Three Musketeers* and beyond, there has always been a body of the *romanesque* which children have claimed as their own, despite preceptorial censorship. We remember Rousseau's description, in the *Confessions,* of how he and his father would stay up all night reading adventure novels; and we know too that all of these novels, with the sole exception of *Robinson Crusoe,* were banished when Rousseau came to the establishment of a pedagogical program for Emile. That is, despite the design given to their literature by adults, and, before that, despite the lack of any literature designated as theirs, children have for centuries made a selection from literature, and possessed certain domains within it.

Before asking how and why this process operates, one is put before the whole question of the *concept* of childhood. For childhood, as Philippe Ariès brilliantly demonstrates in *L'Enfant et la vie familiale sous l'ancien régime,* [1] is not a separate social, moral, and psychological concept much before the seventeenth century. It is not that children were not appreciated, loved, attended to — indeed, they were promiscuously present in adult activities — but that they were not assigned to a special category distinct from adulthood. Before the Renaissance (and well beyond, especially among the people), children up to about the age of seven had little personal identity, a fact surely linked to the high degree of infant mortality: families were used to producing many more infants than would survive childhood, and one could not be considered viable, hence had no *personality,* until he had survived the dangerous early years; then he was expected rapidly to enter adulthood, to display qualities of reasonableness and self-control. In Western Europe, it seems to have been the Reformation and the Counter-Reformation that imposed a separate and special status on childhood, first of all by insisting on the innocence of childhood, thus on the need to separate it from the adult world — especially the world of knowledge of sexual good and evil — its quality as a moral and emotional limbo which must be isolated and given its own norms and functions. This meant a new attention to pedagogy (in France, the "Petites-Ecoles" of the religious orders derive from the Council of Trent), a new moralization of society's treatment of childhood. No doubt one can look beyond Reformation and Counter-Reformation to the rise of capitalism, to the role of the commercial bourgeoisie in the formation of the modern family, with its insistence on the new ideal of privacy. Before the sixteenth or seventeenth centuries, life was more communal than private; this continued to be the case among the people, and also among the court aristocracy, who conceived life as a constant public self-representation. It is the urban middle classes who first promulgate an ideal of the

---

[1] Paris, 1960. Published in English translation as *Centuries of Childhood* (New York, 1962).

family as a self-contained social unit, and of childhood's place within this unit.

A conception of the separateness of childhood, of its innnocence, and of the need to foster this innocence, provides the motive force for a literature of didactic intent written directly for children. We can recognize the first example of such a literature in the picture book of the Moravian bishop Comenius, the *Orbus pictus,* published in 1657. Then, if we sidestep the difficult question (raised by both Marc Soriano and Philippe Ariès in this issue) of whether Perrault's *Contes* were conceived as children's literature, among the first French works in this tradition would be Mme d'Aulnoy's *Contes de fées* (1698), and Fénelon's *Télémaque* (1699), written for the pleasure and mostly the instruction of the Dauphin, while in England Bunyan published *Pilgrim's Progress* in 1676-78. The eighteenth century — which, from Locke to Rousseau, would begin to consider the psychological requirements of the state of childhood — then produced a children's literature of an impeccable moral rectitude in the works of Mme Leprince de Beaumont, Mme de Genlis, and Arnauld Berquin.[2] Their tales unremittingly inculcate good manners, respect for one's elders and noblesse oblige toward one's inferiors, an overwhelming social conservatism. All of which of course is pervasive in the literature written by bourgeois ladies and gentlemen for bourgeois children in the nineteenth century. But by the mid-nineteenth century we nevertheless clearly reach the Golden Age of a literature written for children: an age which has at least partially understood Rousseau's insistence that children are not small adults, which has been conditioned by the mythic Romantic link of the child and natural religion, and has been enriched by rediscovery of national popular literature. This is an age where true writers, from the Comtesse de Ségur to Jules Verne, will turn to children's literature, understanding it as a distinct genre which assigns precise functions and limits to the *dulce* and the *utile,* but which also, because of its conventions and limits, the presumed interests, qualities, insufficiencies, and lacks of its audience,

---

[2] See Paul Hazard's discussion of this literature in his classic *Les Livres, les enfants et les hommes* (Paris, 1932).

can provide a unique vehicle for imaginative play and liberation. The vast, post-Freudian children's literature industry of today has both won new social freedoms, and possibly imposed further interdictions. In its most degraded forms, it has reduced the *dulce* to a small repertory of gags, the *utile* to promotion of a least common denominator of socially acceptable attitudes.

Origins and lines of descent come through with fair clarity, then, when we talk of literature written for children. But when we turn to literature read by children, the question at once becomes more complex. We are first of all faced with a phenomenon of spontaneous age stratification. How is it that certain books written for a normal literary public — that is, for an adult public — become clamped, as it were, into a particular stratum in the growth and aging of mankind?[3] Dumas did not conceive of himself as any different from Balzac in the Republic of Letters; why must we read Dumas as children, or at most as adolescents? Why are Fenimore Cooper's novels, despite all their striving for literary effect, the exclusive province of youth? (I leave aside writers of PhD theses in American Literature.) Why does *Robinson Crusoe* remain a "boy's book"? To be somewhat more problematical, why are the novels of Thomas Wolfe, or Alain-Fournier's *Le Grand Meaulnes,* essentially unreadable after adolescence? Or, in a reverse phenomenon, why are Jules Verne's novels, explicitly and carefully written for boys, now the object of a cult for some of France's most sophisticated literary critics?

A satisfactory answer would no doubt have to take each case individually. Yet the characteristics of the novels mentioned are similar enough to suggest at least the starting point of a more general answer: these novels define themselves as children's literature through a kind of lack, an absence, or perhaps more accurately a sublimation. The genre of the adventure novel defines itself as a world of men pitted against nature or the forces of the universe without the necessary intervention of women — which is true as well, I think, of the genre's

---

[3] Philippe Ariès argues, in the pages of this issue, that the themes of children's literature are originally those themes "abandoned" by adults. This would seem to be true of the literature *given* to children by adults: is it so for the literature which children claim on their own?

earliest forms and precursors, the *Roman de Renart, Robin Hood,* even chivalric romance, where woman is principally the initiator or the end term of a process which excludes her. The world of the adventure novel is essentially pre-pubescent, one where antagonism, confrontations, lure, excitement do not demand, may even explicitly interdict, the presence of women. The interdiction can be read as a sublimation. If one were to analyze the kind of joyous fear evoked by Stevenson's *Treasure Island* — surely one of the masterpieces of womanless fiction — its progressive creation of mystery and suspense, its movement out from the home across the sea to the island, to nightmare and to treasure, one could probably trace the perfect adequation of this tale of adventure to the erotic pursuit. Another example that comes to mind is the great English series *Swallows and Amazons,* by Arthur Ransome, where the adventures lived by a group of vaguely pubescent boys and girls provides an idealized erotic interplay through emulation in heroic gesture (which is partly to say that we are within the cult of the "tom boy," which may be a peculiarly Anglo-Saxon version of acceptable pre-sexual romance).

It is worth dwelling on the adventure tale because, from Arthurian romance through the blue-covered penny dreadfuls known as *littérature de colportage* to the works of Dumas, Marryat, Stevenson, Verne and countless others, it constitutes the material which to generations of young readers has seemed the very essence of the *romanesque,* the purest state of the fictional. By the conventions of the adventure tale, all problematical psychological issues are sublimated to the overt gesture of man in intelligent, controlled, and ieventually successful conflict with the mysterious and daemonic forces of his environment — forces which in adult literature will tend to concentrate in the erotic daemon. (This may explain why Verne, whose fictional conflicts are most explicitly based on man's struggles to master and order the world of contingency through the deployment of his intelligence, seems to create complex allegories of good and evil from the midst of which the banished erotic element reasserts its absent presence.) As the label implies, the adventure tale calls for a world where things happen, and happen in the open, where nothing is hidden, where everything is eventually explainable, where man is victorious over those irrational and mystifying elements in nature (we should read in terms of adult fiction: in himself) which refuse the status of the overt, which menace by their submersion and lack of clarity. If this is so, could we not, reflecting on such books as *Treasure Island, The Mysterious Island,* or even Frances Hodgson Burnett's *The Mysterious Garden,* consider that the child's adventure story is a perfect example of Freud's description of the "familiar" become the "uncanny," the *heimlich* become the *unheimlich*? "The *unheimlich*," says Freud, "is what was once *heimisch*, home-like, familiar; the prefix "un" is the token of repression." [4] Through the play of repression, the adult writing for children consciously or unconsciously, possibly because he is unwilling or unable to assume the burden of adult sexuality, metamorphoses the erotic quest into a quest for adventure which takes the hero far from the *heimisch,* into a world where Woman and Mother are only implicit presences, to do battle with monsters, enigmas, and cataclysms, through his victory to find triumphant peace. Does the child reader unconsciously decode the story, respond to the adventure because he interiorizes the *unheimisch* and feels its relevance to the *heimisch*?

Such speculation leads us to other reflections on repression and imagination in children's literature. The questions that suggest themselves could be posed in different ways. One of them might be this: why did Victorian and Edwardian England, where the public social repression level was probably as high as it has ever been anywhere, produce a children's literature of an unparalleled richness and fantasy? (The French equivalent, the Second Empire and early Third Republic, is both less publicly repressed and less rich imaginatively, but generally similar enough.) The case of C. L. Dodgson / Lewis Carroll is paradigmatic here, as Michael Holquist's article in this issue suggests, but it is not altogether isolated. It is as if childhood, because of the network of interdictions and silences which surrounded it, became for the Victorians and Edwardians the one safe domain for expressing

---

[4] "The Uncanny," (*Das Unheimlich*), translated by Alix Strachey, in *Studies in Parapsychology* (New York: Collier Books, 1963), p. 51.

Peter Brooks

their fantasies: because children are innocent, they are incorruptible, therefore one can say anything to them. Or perhaps more accurately: because the genus of literature for children is *by definition* pure, morally uplifting and innocent, the writer is psychologically free to use it for a maximal liberation of his inner life. More generally, is it perhaps true that because of the presumed innocence of children, their lack of contact with corruption, and the assumed restrictions of any writer addressing himself to them, children's literature gains an equal and (seemingly) opposite liberation of the imagination? Great writers have always used the conventions of any given genre as a source of strength and liberty through constraint; the conventions, the constraints of children's literature are the most specifically moral that there are; great writers adapting to them (indeed, attracted to them) may find them a source of strength, a way of being constrained into liberty. The case could at least be argued for Carroll, for Stevenson, for Verne, for the Comtesse de Ségur.

Related to this question is a still larger problem, the problem of whether children's literature, or let us say a child's reading, somehow accomplishes his apprenticeship in literature and in culture through putting him in contact with the bedrock of fiction, with the archetypal forms of narrative imagination, with supreme fictions. The suspicion that this is so may derive from the fact that children's literature seems in many instances closer to the great unwritten store of folk tale, which would represent man's primary attempt to give meaning to his experience through the making of fictions. When at the end of the seventeenth century Perrault writes down and publishes tales which had been told for indeterminate centuries — and would continue to be told, and would be collected in varying versions by the Grimm Brothers and other modern folklorists — he seems to be performing for children's literature what must have been effected for *literature* long before: that is, he is creating a literature where before there had been myth and folklore. The act of transcription, both creative and destructive, takes us from the primitive to the modern, makes the stories and their themes enter into literacy, into civilization, into history. And children's literature seems to claim a continued close relation to the primitive material through a simplicity of characters, narrative structure and decor which makes us often feel that there is a connection, in the terms Marc Soriano subjects to critical examination, between the "art of childhood" and the "childhood of art." If we take for analysis any of the stories which have a clear appeal to children generation after generation, whether it be Perrault's *Peau d'âne* or Jean de Brunhoff's *Babar le petit éléphant* or *Goldilocks and the Three Bears* (a tale first transcribed in 1834) or a more recent book like Maurice Sendak's *Where the Wild Things Are,* we find narratives of a simplicity and strength which it is difficult to duplicate without going back to Greek tragedy. If one were to analyze them in detail, one could (somewhat pedantically) inventory essential narrative procedures, show repeated binary and ternary patterns both in characters and in narrative situations, demonstrate the omnipresent encounter of beauty and the beast, the purgative role of fear, the educative role of fear understood and dominated. Above all, I think, one would be made aware of the extent to which everything is subordinated to narrative fictionalizing, the way any didactic intent, any characterization, any metaphor or symbolism, is held in check by a desire to make the tale do all the work. [5] Of relevance here would also be the traditional and seemingly spontaneous forms of expression "invented" by children themselves: rhymes, *comptines,* riddles, and so forth: a kind of zero-degree literature in which we can seize the work of the imagination as mediator between consciousness and the world of phenomena. [6]

We may be on the verge of falling into a Romantic delusion, and assuming that the fiction of the *Volk* is both more childish and more true than later, more sophisticated ("sentimental," in Schiller's terminology) fictions. Yet there clearly is a sense in which the art of childhood *is* the childhood of art: in the very obvious sense that the literature a child reads is his apprenticeship in reading, his appren-

---

[5] This would seem to me to be true also in the nonsense of Carroll and Lear, who always maintain a strong narrative line *within* the nonsensical, so that the sense that derives from progression is never lost. As Alice comments after reading "Jabberwocky," "*somebody* killed *something*: that's clear, at any rate..."

[6] See Marc Soriano's article in this issue. See also Iona and Peter Opie, *The Lore and Language of Schoolchildren* (Oxford, 1960).

ticeship in fictionmaking, in society's legitimized forms of the imaginary. When Alice asks the Mock Turtle what he was taught in school, his list, taking in "Reeling and Writhing," "Ambition, Distraction, Uglification, and Derision," "Mystery, ancient and modern," "Drawling, Stretching, and Fainting in Coils," ends with the Classical master's subjects, "Laughing and Grief." After we register the pun on Latin and Greek, we uncover the profundity of the remark: Laughing and Grief — like the other attitudes and acts of the list — are things that we learn, things that are taught to us as children by the adult world. [7] And so it is with our sense of the fictional, our sense of what constitutes a story, of what elements properly belong in a narrative, of what "character" is like, of what constitutes beginnings and ends, climaxes and resolutions. Any child with a reasonably extensive experience of literature soon becomes positively an Aristotelean when it comes to plots: he can immediately spot variations, violations of an almost classical *vraisemblance*. And this *vraisemblance*, like Boileau's, has to do not so much with what experience dictates to us as with the laws of fabulation, of fictionmaking — a distinct activity, related to the life-material it uses, but independent of it. A child who has read *Treasure Island* has received an entire education in the processes and laws of the *romanesque*, of the kind of lying which we call imaginative creation.

The importance of lying is what it finally comes down to. Plato exiled the poets, Bossuet and other clerics of the seventeenth and eighteenth centuries condemned novels and sought to censor them, because they felt that fabulation, "make-believe," the imaginary — in a word, lying — was by its nature unhealthy and corrupting. Rousseau's puritan naturalism in *Emile* confirms the judgment: the fictional is essentially corrupt and corrupting. In a sense, these censors who condemned all literature were the true critics, because they best recognized the power of fabulation. The literature written for children, and especially the literature written for anyone but claimed and appropriated by children, provides a proof in reverse, a proof that the fiction-making capacity is preserved, fostered, and learned by each new

---

[7] I am grateful to my friend John Hollander for first pointing this out to me.

generation. And if there is a tendency on the part of many of those professionally committed to children's literature to resist the brave new McLuhanite para-literary world, it is probably not so much that they feel television and other audio-visual media to fail in their didactic function — on the contrary, they are in many ways incomparable transmitters of information — but because these media have so far provided no new forms of apprenticeship in the imaginary to replace that conveyed by books. As the Swiss historian of children's literature, Bettina Hürlimann, argues, [8] the comic strip reduces language to a mere legend, a kind of stereotyped naming of what is going on in the frame of the picture (whereas between the legend under an etching by one of Verne's illustrators and the picture itself there was a complex and enriching dialogue). So far—and Freud's whole enterprise confirms this — men have found few media more powerful than language to express their imaginative reformation of reality. We must continue to teach lying.

---

[8] Bettina Hürlimann, *Three Centuries of Children's Books in Europe,* translated by Brian W. Alderson (London, 1967), pp. 169-70.

Philippe Ariès

At the point of origin

Books addressed to and reserved for children appear at the end of the 17th century, at the same time as the awareness of childhood. For about two centuries printing presses had increasingly produced editions of ancient and modern texts, disseminated among a new and wider public the habit of reading; children were excluded from this public, at least "children" as a separate category, although more and more of them were going to schools and Latin regencies, and they were beginning to constitute an age group characterized by its own code of behavior. But all this was just beginning, and adults had not yet had the time to realize it.

Thanks to some recent works, we can now guess how these adults became concerned with children to the point of writing books exclusively for them.

In order for the necessary distancing between the adult's and child's world to take place, children had to be sufficiently separated from adults by boarding schools, in a world apart. It was also necessary that the themes offered to them cease to be those of adults and, so abandoned, become "available."

In fact, this handing down to children of themes common to all of society took place in two separate stages. First, at the end of the sixteenth century and during the first half of the seventeenth century, the new nobility, the men of the Robe, gave up the old fund of the "marvellous" which had nourished medieval literature. The extraordinary stories of Morgane the fairy, Merlin the magician, Melusine, the Knights of the Round Table, gallant and chivalrous adventures, had belonged to the repertory of the aristocratic courts and also to the repertory of the people; they were the same myths, products of an ancient and yet very present folklore, which enchanted rich and poor, young and old, educated clerics and illiterate peasants. Don Quixote was still mad about them, but it was found that they went to his head and kept him from being taken seriously.

In a little book written in 1614, *La manière de lire l'histoire,* René de Lusinge tells how he began, at the age of twelve, by reading Huon de Bordeaux, the four Aymon sons, Pierre de Provence and Maguelone, Ogier le Danois. When he became a "learned doctor in this fabulous science," he "took on all the Amadis des Gaules." "This chimaeric science on the value of his paladins transported me out of myself and left me no liberty to do anything else night or day; I devoured them in no time at all."

The upper class soon had stopped reading these old fables. Henceforth they read something else: classical French literature, tragedy, comedy, and especially the novel, the endless novel — *Clélie, L'Astrée.* In his charming book *De la culture populaire au XVIIe et XVIIIe siècle,* [1] Robert Mandrou has shown how the medieval verse chronicle, chivalry cycles, fused with the tradition of oral folklore, had been preserved by popular story tellers, and how the memory and imagination of these storytellers had been helped and passed on by the little books of the *Bibliothèque bleue,* "bleue" because they were bound with blue paper. The medieval repertory always constituted the largest part of this popular literature which was sold at fairs and marketplaces by peddlers: a culture which was hence mainly rural. The common people of the towns undoubtedly shared the disaffection of their masters.

We already knew that this popular literature of medieval origin became the literature of the children of the upper classes, [2] but we did not know how. It seemed only that the nurses, the foster brothers, the young valets who were companions in the early childhood years always told the same stories to the young nobles or bourgeois, who were delighted with them. This mixing with the servants well explains

---

[1] Paris, 1965.
[2] This is what I tried to show in the chapter on youth in *L'Enfant et la vie familiale* (Paris, 1960).

Philippe Ariès

the persistence of the oral tradition among the masters' children, but not how this tradition furnished the material for a literature written especially for them, and completely different from the literature of the peddlers.

The passage from oral story telling to children's books is made in France with the stories of the *Contes du temps passé,* generally attributed to Charles Perrault, which appeared in 1697. Since today we are aware of the extraordinary popularity of the tales of Perrault among numerous generations of children, we are tempted to find it absolutely normal that one day an Academician, and perhaps his son of 16 or 17, should have decided to write what had never before been written, a book for children, thus creating a literature and, at the same time, an industry. Was it Perrault's intention, or was it rather the subsequent uninterrupted success of two centuries' duration, that made these tales a book for children?

We are now well informed about Perrault and his family by an interesting and strange book, one which combines precious information, ingenious ideas, and psychoanalytic abberations: *Les Contes de Perrault,* by Marc Soriano.[3]

The tales of Perrault, along with those of Mme d'Aulnoy and Mlle Lheritier, belong to a literary fashion which has been well studied by M. E. Storer.[4] The tales were directed at adult members of good society. Leibniz had no doubts about this when he wrote in 1716: "People are bored with reasonable novels such as the French *Clélie,* the German *Armene;* and for some time they have come back to reading fairy tales." Fairy tales, which never ceased to nourish the popular literature of the peddlers. It had not been such a long time since people had abandoned them, and one can see that there was a certain nostalgia in the return, no doubt for the reasons given by Leibniz: "It is one of man's misfortunes that he becomes weary of reason itself, and bored with the light of truth. Chimaeras come back and are welcomed once again, because they are of the realm of the marvellous."

---

[3] Paris, 1968.
[4] *La mode des contes de fées (1685-1700)* (Paris, 1920).

But at the end of a century of rationality the "chimaeras" could no longer "return" without an alibi, and *the child furnished that alibi*: this is the essential fact.

"In this respect," observes M. Soriano, "it is interesting to notice that Mlle. Lheritier and Perrault are always talking about 'old wives' tales,' 'governesses' and guardians' tales.' Are they unaware that this repertory, almost in its entirety, is addressed to adults and not to children? It seems unlikely. In the seventeenth century folklore was part of reality, belonging to the daily life of the people. Unambiguous texts in which Perrault talks of popular superstitions are addressed to adults. Why, in this case, does he pretend to believe they are for children?"

Why? Because, if folklore is part of *contemporary* reality for the people, it dates from *yesterday,* from gothic barbarism, for the upper classes. It is, moreover, remarkable that in the *Parallèle des anciens et des modernes,* Perrault, in praise of the Moderns, had the idea of comparing the fables of Antiquity and the Homeric poems with our "old wives' tales," the "tales of *Peau d'Ane* and Mother Goose."

But why then did Perrault and Mlle Lheritier pretend to have written these stories for children when they were in fact addressed to adults? That is the real question. "I found myself," wrote Mlle Lheritier in 1695 at the latest, "in the company of some very distinguished people when the conversation turned to poems, tales and short stories. We stopped often to talk about this last kind of work: we examined its divers characteristics, in verse, in prose." They came to Perrault, who had already published two tales in verse. Mlle Lheritier felt obliged to remark that "however beautiful such works might be, they were nonetheless the least works that had come from the pen of that illustrious author."

Mlle Lheritier had to explain why this illustrious author had come to be interested in old wives tales. "We talked of the *fine education* he gives his children, we noted that all of them show much intelligence, and finally we came to the naive tales that one of his young students (his son) had recently written down with such charm. We told several of them and this naturally led to telling others. I had to tell one when

Philippe Ariès

it was my turn..." We will leave Mlle Lheritier telling "the one about Marmoisan, with some embellishments which came to me on the spur of the moment." Once again we find proof that the old tradition of telling tales in society had not been completely lost, even among "people of distinction." What one must notice in this text is the alibi used by Mlle Lheritier for Perrault: "the fine education he gives his children." Like so many in this end of the seventeenth century, at the start of the great movement which will go from Locke's *On the Education of Children* to *Emile* and the psychological and pedagogical reforms of the 18th century, Perrault is interested in education. He talks about it in the *Parallèle des Anciens et des Modernes*. He also talks about it in the Preface of the *Contes en vers*: "Is it not praiseworthy that mothers and fathers, when their children are not yet capable of tasting solid truths devoid of all sweetening, make them love these truths, and as it were, swallow them, by enclosing them in agreeable tales proportioned to the weakness of their age." "It is not believable with what avidity these innocent souls... assimilate these hidden lessons; they are sad, they are deep in grief when the hero or heroine of the tale is unfortunate."

This is well observed. There is a great difference in attitudes toward children between the end of the seventeenth century and the reigns of Henry IV and Louis XIII. Elsewhere I have given examples of how little attention and respect was given to children and their lives at the time of Montaigne and during the youth of Louis XIII. [5] This remains true still longer among the people; in his commonplace book, a cloth merchant from Lille, who was born around 1633 and died in 1693, and who has been studied recently, mentions the death of his mother, speaks twice of a cousin who was a nun and of her death, notes the unexpected arrival of another cousin who left one day thirty years before for Germany: there is not a word about his own children. It took the erudition of his historian to discover that he had at least three. [6]

---

[5] *L'Enfance et la vie familiale*, p. 29, 101.
[6] A. Lottin, *Vie et mentalité d'un Lillois sous Louis XIV* (Lille, 1968).

At the point of origin

The upper class at the end of the period of Louis XIV shows, on the contrary, a very modern sentiment towards children. Racine follows the studies of his son Louis with the solicitude of a modern parent, inquires about his health, his situation. Similarly Charles Perrault saw to his children's work and told them educational stories. A letter of his from 1689 speaks of a trip he made to Verneuil to "put one of [his] children, whose arm was broken by a fall, into the hands of a M. de Boulay, admirable for his skill in putting broken members back together." [7]

In the new sentimental climate of that generation, it had become normal that a father spend time "giving pleasure to his children" in order to raise them better. The alibi of Perrault, improbable and unthinkable a half-century before, was henceforth admissible: the Abbé Dubos understands it thus in a letter to Bayle who, from his exile, interested himself in Perrault: "the same publisher also prints the *Contes de ma mère l'oye* by M. Perrault. These are the bagatelles with which he used to amuse his children." But Dubos is not a dupe: he knows perfectly well that these tales were addressed to adults when he writes later, "Madame Daunoy is adding a second volume to the Mother Goose tales of M. Perrault. Our century has become quite infantile as far as books are concerned: it needs tales, fables, novels and little stories." That is to say, works of imagination.

One then comes to wonder if the alibi was not in fact more truthful than people claimed to believe, and if the tales ostensibly written for adults had not really been "set down," as one said coquettishly, for that recently invented creature, the child?

Adult? Child? Even the attribution of the *Contes* is ambiguous. Perrault had them appear under the signature of one of his sons, Pierre Darmancour. What could be more natural, one might think, and what could better justify the idea of a book for children? A book for children, written by a child. This was believed for a long time, it is believed still. There is only one drawback: the young

---

[7] All the quotations from Perrault are taken from Soriano's study.

Philippe Ariès

supposed author was no longer a child, neither when he published the *Contes* at the age of nineteen, nor when he supposedly wrote them, around the age of seventeen. A boy of sixteen or seventeen was then older and closer to adults than he is today. Seclusion in schooling had not yet produced all its effects. The future "pacha" of Bonneval set to sea at the age of eleven on the King's ships. At thirteen he was an ensign. Chevert went into the service at the age of eleven. At sixteen Descartes and le Grand Condé had finished school and were living like men.

This was also true for girls, and a girl of fifteen could easily pass as marriageable:

> Le sorcier en fit une fille
> De l'âge de quinze ans et telle et si gentille,
> Que le fils de Priam pour elle aurait tenté
> Plus encore qu'il ne fit pour la grecque beauté.
>
> The witch made a girl
> Age fifteen, and so very nice
> That the son of Priam for her would have dared
> Even more than he did for the Greek beauty.

At sixteen or seventeen one had passed beyond the age of fairies and magic. The young prodigies were tempted rather by other inspirations. Moreover, let us not forget that a bit more than two centuries later and within a social system which less favored precocity, Rimbaud wrote "Le Bateau ivre" at the age of seventeen.

So Pierre Darmancour was no longer a child to whom his nurse told *Peau d'Ane* or *le Petit Poucet*. It is undoubtedly just for this reason that it was decently possible to attribute to him a modern and literary version.

But now, thanks to M. Soriano, we know that the young prodigy was also a rake who was hot-blooded and had a swift sword. Here is what a friend of the family writes in 1697: "His younger son, who is only sixteen or seventeen, having drawn his sword against a neighbour of the same age, an only son, whom he killed in defending himself." Defending himself? That is the version of the Perraults. We can just as well imagine that it was he who picked the fight. It is not necessary to have recourse, in the manner of M. Soriano, to modern theories of psychiatry and juvenile delinquency to explain this mortal fight; the school annals of the seventeenth century are full of acts of violence and children's duels: formerly, children — school boys — fought like adults.

It was perhaps because of this accident that Perrault's son took refuge in the armies. In March, 1700, he was killed in battle, like so many other young nobles of his generation, only three years after the publication of the *Contes en prose* under his name. This tragic but banal destiny underlines the ambiguity of the origins of a book which would become the everpresent ancestor of children's literature.

That the *Contes* were written for children is no longer in doubt in the eighteenth-century and thereafter; success has made the decision. But if children's books are read and accepted by children, they are also chosen and suggested by adults.

The children of the end of the seventeenth century and eighteenth century listened with delight to the tales of their nurses and, moreover, in the Germany of Grimm story tellers often mixed in details invented by Perrault — father or son. But this was a popular and oral literature, previous to the moral reform of the seventeenth-century: like Latin before the Jesuits, the popular language violated "decency." The tales of Perrault preserved the themes and the adventures which delighted the country people and the servants and the children of the masters: nothing better had been invented to captivate their imaginations. But he expurgated them, he got rid of their primitive paganism, he erased the cannibalism from Little Red Riding Hood, transformed the erotic sleep of Sleeping Beauty, the ritual undressing of the wife of Bluebeard. He made the old cruel and savage folklore "proper" and acceptable to the most stringent educators, but without himself dabbling in educative morality. He was not content to preserve the thread of the marvellous adventures which enchanted our ancestors; he added his own special humor, falsely naive, which has delighted children from the

Philippe Ariès

eighteenth-century to the present time, but he delighted them only because he had the consent of parents. The *Contes* are at the source of the image which the adults of the eighteenth and nineteenth centuries created of childhood, innocent and roguish, serious and naive: the "good little devil" of the Comtesse de Ségur.

Translated by Margaret Brooks.

Marc Soriano

From tales of warning to formulettes: the oral tradition in French children's literature

The few studies of children's literature which have been published in France [1] hardly touch on works in the oral tradition. Nonetheless, for centuries storytelling was the only form of artistic expression which reached the great majority of French children. [2] If by chance these studies do consent to mention the oral repertory, they essentially confine theselves to fairy tales, to those stories commonly known in the seventeenth century as *contes de vieilles* (old wives tales), or *contes de mie* (friendly tales), as if they were literature transmitted by "grannies" and deliberately intended for children. But that is not at all the case. These stories are almost entirely directed at an adult audience. To be convinced, one need only read most of them in their unadapted versions, as we find them for example in the large collections of the nineteenth and twentieth centuries. Very often they contain vulgarities, witticisms or scenes of horror which require a certain sophistication on the part of the audience in order to be understood or appreciated.

Yet the criterion of "decency" was established in France only with the missions of the Counter-Reformation in the sixteenth and seventeenth centuries, and even then it did not have the same stringent and obligatory character in the country and among the lower classes that it did in the cities, among well-to-do, cultivated people.

---

[1] Including, alas, my *Guide de la littérature enfantine* (Flammarion, 1959) which, partly because of this lack, I consider to be completely out of date.

[2] At least until the Guizot Law on Primary Instruction in 1833, and perhaps even until the school laws of the Third Republic. See, on this subject, the fine book by Maurice Contard: *L'Enseignement primaire en France de la Révolution à la Loi Guizot (1789-1833)*, (Lyon, 1959); and the more recent synthesis by Antoine Prost, *L'Enseignement en France 1800-1967* (Armand Colin, "Collection U," 1968).

Marc Soriano

Peasant children were raised in contact with the realities of existence, in the promiscuity of misery and ignorance. Even before Perrault legalized it in 1695 in a "modernist" spirit (in his preface to the collection, *Contes en vers* [3]) the amalgam of the children's and the popular repertory must already have existed.

It didn't occur to parents to keep the children from listening during those long evenings when someone told those fabulous stories which were not particularly meant for their ears. And usually the children — for want of something better, perhaps — enjoyed them. The dramatic action, the extraordinary adventures which filled them made them at least partly assimilable by young minds. It all came about as if this "childhood of art" through some sort of spontaneous alchemy was transformed into "art of childhood." In fact this is not true, and one of the most delicate tasks of contemporary pedagogy must be to separate out the components of this faulty alloy. [4]

We should avoid this error so much the more that oral literature does include a number of stories destined specifically for children. These include certain "animal stories," "tales of warning," and most of that sort of nursery rhymes the French call *formulettes*. In this brief study I shall limit myself to giving a general idea of the vast repertory of these true children's stories, and to establishing its boundaries.

* * *

As far as one can tell, the "animal stories" made up a literature of transition which was quite naturally common to both adults and children. We know that Renard's wicked deeds were greatly enjoyed by the peasants and simple village folk, who undoubtedly

---

[3] Preface to the fourth edition of *Griselidis,* followed by *Peau d'Ane* and the short story, *Les Souhaits ridicules,* Paris, 1695.

[4] Indeed, teachers and parents often say in good faith, "what was good enough for us should be good enough for our children and for their children." This is partly true, and there is no need to rush out and destroy traditions. Still, we should keep in mind that psychology and psychoanalysis have been born and developed, and that our educational criteria have been refined. The children of the Old Régime also lived without vaccines and antibiotics. It seems to me that one of the tasks of teachers today is to make a selection from this vast repertory, using the criteria of our time.

enriched the stories with social and political chords. But they also pleased the children, who, as Henri Wallon has astutely remarked, [5] have a tendency to sympathize with animals, perhaps because they live on the same scale, and to identify with animals of the same size that they are, which might reasonably be one of the causes of the current popularity of "animal art" among young audiences.

Le Roman de Renard is the most typical and successful of the *summae* of animal stories. But is it really a book for children? It seems to me that this work, stuffed with political and social allusions which require an understanding of masses of precise historic allusions, and including some frankly licentious episodes, notwithstanding its role as one of the finest and most important products of our literature, has ceased to be appropriate for children, or in any case for very young ones. However, it becomes a wonderful book for children again very easily, if meticulous, scrupulous writers take the trouble either to adapt it, or to present coherent extracts which correspond to the levels of comprehension of various age groups. [6]

* * *

It has only been a short time since the importance of the "warning tales" as a separate current of oral literature was recognized. The great French folklorist, Paul Delarue, was the first investigator to recognize this clearly, in an important series of articles published in the *Bulletin Folklorique d'Ile de France,* in 1952. His hypothesis has been the basis for a number of studies, such as that of Marianne Rumph in Germany: *Little Red Riding Hood and the Tales of Warning.* The Danish folklore expert Rubow examined Danish folklore with identical preoccupations in 1955.

---

[5] Preface to the special number of *Enfance* devoted to children's books, 1956.
[6] There are several good adaptations in French. Père Castor (Paul Faucher), one of the great pioneers of children's literature in France, who died in 1967, edited several episodes intended for beginning readers (published by Flammarion). A broader adaptation, meant for readers in the ten to fifteen year-old age group, has been prepared by Leopold Chaveau for La Farandole, and there is another by Guillot, which won the Andersen prize. Finally, I must mention a fine complete translation-adaptation by Maurice Genevoix, which is appropriate for both adolescents and adults.

Marc Soriano

The first research to be undertaken — and it is still very fragmentary — shows that there are a great many "tales of warning" in France. This label can be applied to all those stories whose purpose is to divert children from menacing dangers such as water, the forest, etc. So that the syncretic and anthropomorphic mind of the child can assimilate the lesson, the story *materializes* the danger by populating the tale with wild animals or troubling personages, which means that *monsters become associated with dangerous places*. These boogeymen, sea monsters and other terrifying characters (to whom Delarue has consecrated a veritable bibliography in the work cited above) are reputed to lurk in these dangerous areas in wait for children, to draw them into their lairs and devour them.

I came upon the basic process of development of these stories completely accidentally one day, upon hearing my wife (who at the time had no particular knowledge of folklore) explain to my youngest daughter that she mustn't lean out the window, because behind the shutter there lived a horrible old lady, "Mrs. Gravity," who grabbed little children and dragged them to the ground with amazing speed. This process, one notices, was already contaminated with the scientific terminology of our time.

The best known of the "warning tales" in France is and always has been *Little Red Riding-Hood*. I shall not go into it in depth here, since I just made a long study of it in my book, *Les Contes de Perrault, culture savante et traditions populaires*. The versions of this story in the oral tradition which can be collected today have, not surprisingly, frequently undergone the influence of the version attributed to Perrault. Those which precede or are independent of Perrault (there are some) can be recognized by a certain number of characteristics which have continued to survive in spite of the celebrity of the text published in 1967: the motif of cruelty — probably a reflection of a "primitive structure" — the motif of the blood and flesh of the grandmother which are placed on the bread-bin and which the little girl is invited to eat; the motif of the "familiar animal" — a cat or bird (or mysterious voice) which informs the child of what she is eating; the episode of the "ritual undressing," a sort of strip-tease by Little Red Riding-Hood, who each time she takes off a garment asks the wolf where she should put it, which leads to an enigmatic or frankly menacing response from the ferocious animal; and finally, a "happy ending" of a particular type, built on the scatological overtone of the "tie which sets free": the little girl pretends that she urgently needs to relieve herself, a pretext to escape from the monster. He, suspicious but slow-witted, gives in at last, after having taken the precaution of attaching her to a cord, from which she frees herself forthwith.

The wide diffusion of this tale in print should not make us forget that there exist many others of the same type which are themselves very pretty and greatly enjoyed by children: for example that of *La Chèvre et les chevreaux*, whose old age is certified by the well-known fable by La Fontaine, [7] which concludes with the ancient proberb in Picard dialect:

> *Biaux Chires Loups, n'écoutez mie,*
> *Mère tenchant chen fieux qui crie.*

> My fine lord wolf please pay no mind
> While a mother scolds her son who whines.

Paul Delarue remarks with perspicacity on the subject of these frightening creatures that "the monsters with which we threaten children to keep them away from water are especially numerous and varied, whereas to make them afraid of woods and paths leading into them, there is really only one monster which has remained traditionally the same for centuries and centuries: the wolf, terror of adults and children alike, the wolf who has in fact carried off and devoured so many children." [8]

In spite of their diversity, all these stories have an identical structure which is explained by the effect sought: simple rhythyms,

---

[7] *Fables,* Book IV, 16.
[8] Paul Delarue, *Bulletin folklorique d'Ile de France,* Oct.-Dec. 1951, p. 290.

Pl. 2 Petit Chaperon rouge,

formulae punctuating the climatic moments, dramatic dialogue which announces the imminent catastrophe and intensifies the "suspense."

Some may find it surprising that the only stories of the traditional repertory which are aimed directly at children should be precisely those with unhappy endings. Nonetheless, that is the way it is, and this apparent paradox should not be immediately written off with an hypothesis of "cruelty" in children. The true reason is simpler. Even though these stories are presented as tales "purely for amusement," they actually belong to educational literature, or better, *functional* literature. They take on meaning as soon as one recognizes their purpose, which is to *frighten* the child.

It is true that in the end, certain children come to find pleasure in fear and cruelty. Adults themselves may be tempted to abuse this easy, all too effective teaching method. The warning tales pose some pedagogical problems which we ought to look at in the light of the contemporary behavioral sciences. It is interesting to note that the "pedagogy of fear" was already criticized at the time of Perrault. A "song" by *le petit Coulanges,* a relative and friend of Madame de Sévigné who frequented the same aristocratic and bourgeois salons as Perrault, furnishes us with a proof which is not lacking in color: [9]

> ... En faveur des petits enfants
> Je veux gronder les gouvernantes
> Qui pour les rendre obéissants
> Leur font des peurs extravagantes
> Et qui, contentes du succès,
> Les rendent peureux à jamais.
>
> On leur fait peur du loup garou,
> On leur fait peur de la grand'bête;
> Le dragon va sortir d'un trou
> Qui pour les avaler s'apprête.

---

[9] *Avis aux pères de famille* to the tune of *Les Ennuyeux*. (In *Chansons Choisies,* ed. M. de Coulanges, 2 volumes, 1968.)

Marc Soriano

> Enfin ces petits malheureux
> N'ont que des monstres autour d'eux. ...

> To speak out for the little child
> I feel that I must scold the nurse.
> For to keep him meek and mild
> She threatens with a monster curse,
> And happy to have calmed the strife
> Leaves him fearful all his life.
>
> He's haunted by the boogey-man;
> He's haunted by the werewolf's cry.
> The dragon's coming from his den
> To gulp him down. And by and by
> The frightened child is weak and cowed,
> Surrounded by a monster crowd...

The theme and the structure of the "warning tales" have left their mark on our literature. They reappear in more elaborate, more or less contaminated forms in several of the major children's books, like *La Chèvre de Monsieur Seguin,* one of the most famous and beloved of children's stories, in the *Lettres de mon moulin* by Alphonse Daudet, in *Le Château des loups,* a very fine story published around ten years ago by Henri Troyat.

* * *

Another important part of the oral repertory intended for children is the childhood nursery rhyme or *formulette.* This collective expression seems appropriate to designate that "literature of rhymes and games" which, says Eugène Rolland (author of the first large collection of these poems [10]), "children have transmitted to one another

---

[10] Eugène Rolland, *Rimes et jeux de l'enfance* (Paris: Masonneuve et Cie., 1883; reëdition, 1968), p. 396.

throughout history, which is the only literature that amuses them, the only one appropriate to their mental development, and which is totally different from that which our "utilitarian" teachers would have them learn at any price."

This very ancient literary form (we find traces of it in Rabelais and in a great many texts of popular inspiration [11]) has only recently begun to be studied. For the last century, compulsory education and the influence of the printed text have certainly weakened and altered it; but in spite of these factors of decomposition, it remains an extremely tenacious and living form of literature, particularly because it belongs to an age group where the child does not yet know how to read, or at any rate has not yet mastered the mechanics of rapid reading, and where his memory is particularly fresh. Another factor which facilitates the transmission of these rhymes is their association with games teaching motor control or more generally with games transmitted by women (mothers and grandmothers, the first educators) who in our civilization still constitute the most stable and, by necessity, the most traditionalist element.

Both modern pedagogy and the Surrealist movement, by recognizing the exceptional artistic quality of this "involuntary poetry," have facilitated the conservation effort. Educators and some contemporary poets, such as Philippe Soupault, Robert Desnos, Raymond Queneau and Claude Roy, have been interested in these *formulettes,* collecting them and imitating them. [12] Certain studies have been made by men like Joisten, [13] or Philippe Soupault and Jean Bacaumont for the French radio, [14] and they have brought together an impressive number of the rhymes.

---

[11] I have found many traces in the early poems by the Perrault brothers, particularly in their parody of Book VI of the *Aeneid.*

[12] A great number of them have been collected in the journals printed by children in the experimental schools directed by Freinet, or according to his method. André Bay and Claude Roy on the one hand, and the psychologist Jean Chateau on the other, have published anthologies.

[13] Charles Joisten, "*La Vie traditionnelle enfantine dans les Hautes Alpes, enquête folklorique*" Spring 1951-Winter 1953 and Spring-Winter 1954, *Bulletin de la Société d'Études Historiques des Hautes Alpes,* nos. 45 and 46, pp. 44-51, 103-105, Gap, 1953-54.

[14] *Les Comptines de la langue française,* collected and commented by J. Bacaumont, Seghers, 1961, p. 366.

Marc Soriano

These collections use a mass of classifications based in some cases on the internal structure of the poems, in others on the presence or absence of puns, alliteration, etc. These linguistic distinctions are certainly very useful, but for the historian of children's literature, they have the drawback of making one forget that these little texts belong first to the category of *functional literature*. To me, the apparently more capricious classification by Eugène Rolland shows greater awareness of this reality. He makes it clear that these little works follow step by step the development of "small mankind" from his birth to the moment he leaves childhood. They rock him to sleep, make his first movements rhythmic, transforming them into games. Here, for example, is the Breton formulette which "explains" to a baby the circular movement of hands, by making them into puppets:

> *Dansez, dansez bell'main,*
> *Vous aurez du gâteau demain.* (bis)
> *Ah! la bell'main, la menette,*
> *Ah! la bell'main que j'ai!*
>
> (from the region around Lorient, E. Rolland, p. 17)

> Dance, dance, pretty hand,
> Tomorrow you shall have some cake. (repeat)
> Oh my pretty hand, my little pretty hand,
> Oh that pretty hand of mine!

There is another Breton *formulette* to permit inspection of the various parts of the face:

> *Menton forchu - Bouche d'argent - Nez cancan - Joue bouillie - Joue rôtie - Œil de Picard - Œil de St. Martin - Tape, tape sur le robin.*
>
> (Finistère, *Ibid.,* p. 19)

From tales of warning to formulettes

Cleft chin, silver mouth, tattling nose, boiling cheek, roasting cheek, Picard eye, Saint Martin's eye, - Tap, tap on the snoot.

and one for the fingers of the hand:

> *Celui-ci a vu le lièvre - celui-ci l'a couru - celui-ci l'a tenu - celui-ci l'a mangé - celui-là n'a rien eu - il a dit à sa mère:*
> *—Je n'ai pas eu, je n'ai pas eu.*
>
> (Lorient)

This one saw the hare; this one chased it; this one caught it; this one ate it; that one didn't get any. He said to his mother: "I didn't get any, I didn't get any!" *

There are *formulettes* to make a crying child laugh, to make him hold still, to tickle him, etc. The greatest part of this literature is associated with games. There are round-dances, like that of the oats:

> *Qui veut ouir, qui veut savoir*
> *Comme on sème l'avoine* (ici on imite le semeur)
> *Mon per' la semait ainsi,*
> *Puis se reposait un p'tit,*
> *Tapait des pieds, battait des mains*
> *Et faisait le tour du vilain.*
> *Avoine, avoine, avoine,*
> *Le beau temps te ramène.*
>
> (Region around Paris, E. Rolland, p. 100)

If you want to hear, if you want to know
How to sow the oats (here an imitation of the sower)

---

* *Translator's note*: The English equivalent for many of these poems will be evident to the reader. The English toe-counting game, "This little Pig went to Market" is very similar to this one.

34

Marc Soriano

    My father sowed them like this,
    Then he rested a little bit,
    Tapped his feet, clapped his hands,
    And went the round of the peasant man.
    Oats, oats, oats, oats, oats, oats, oats, oats, oats,
    Sunshine brings you back again. *

There is also the roundelay of the "doctor and the kisses," which no doubt comes back into fashion at a less innocent age:

    Donne-moi le bras que je te guérisse,
    Car tu m'as l'air malade (bis)
        Lonla,
    Car tu m'as l'air malade!

(pointing out a person of the opposite sex):

    Embrasse monsieur (ou madame) pour te guérir
    C'est un fort bon remède. (bis)
        Lonla,
    C'est un fort bon remède.

                      (*Ibid.* p. 76)

    Give me your arm so I can cure you
    'Cause you look sick to me (repeat)
        Tra-la
    'Cause you look sick to me!

(pointing out a person of the opposite sex):

---

   * English has many "action" games like this. A similar one is "Here We go round the Mulberry Bush".

> Kiss this nice man (or lady) so you get well
> That is the best cure of all (repeat)
> > Tra-la
> That is the best cure of all.

Another variety of *formulette* is the little song called *menterie* ("tall tale") which corresponds to the age where the child begins to have negative judgment permitting him to differentiate and specify his ideas:

> *Ah! j'ai vu, j'ai vu.*
> *Compère, qu'as-tu vu?*
> *J'ai vu une grenouille*
> *Qui filait sa quenouille*
> *Au bord d'un fossé.*
> *—Compère, vous mentez.*

(Ibid. p. 108)

> Oh, I saw something, I saw something.
> Hey pal, what'd you see?
> I saw a frog,
> Sawing a log
> Over the edge of a stream.
> Hey pal, you're lying to me.

The *randonné* (a sort of circular poem, like "The House that Jack Built," or "As I was going to Saint-Ives") is another type of "functional" poem. It enumerates the succession of causes and effects of a particular event: causes and effects which augment, then diminish, teaching the child without his noticing that events (or ideas) are generally logically linked together.

Many of the *formulettes* called *comptines* (counting games) are meant to teach a child to count, an extremely serious operation at the age where he is trying, even in his games, to describe and inventory

Marc Soriano

the world. Jean Bacaumont remarks that this is a "preliminary to all games, a prelude accomplished ritually with attention and gravity to admit players to the game and to choose the beginner by chance, through the intervention of an occult power recognized by all and charged with a sort of oracular decision."

> *Am, stram, gram*
> *Pic et pic et colegram,*
> *Bourre et bourre et rataplam*
> *Am, stram, gram.* *

There seem to be *formulettes* for every occasion. Here is one for a malingerer:

> *Il a la fièvre de mouton;*
> *Ce qu'il mange, il le trouve bon.*
>
> (Poitou, *Ibid.*, p. 257)

> He's got sheep-fever;
> He's still a big eater.

one for anger:

> *Bisque, bisque, rage,*
> *Mange du fromage;*
> *Si le fromage n'est pas bon,*
> *Mange de la poison.*
>
> (Quercy, *Ibid.*, p. 274)

---

* *Translator's note*: This is untranslatable. The English equivalent would be: "Eeney, meeney, miney, moe," etc.

> Spite, spite, rage,
> Have a little cheese.
> If you don't like cheese,
> Eat some poison, please.

and one for boredom:

> *Je m'ennuie, je ne sais pas quoi faire.*
> *Prends un marteau et tape-toi sur les doigts.*
>
> (*Ibid.*, p. 275)

> I'm so bored, I don't know what to do.
> Go take a hammer and beat on your hand.

There is also one of pure verbiage, where the poem seems to get carried away with itself, but which, in spite of that, is not "art for art's sake" or simple verbal juggling, because it contains descriptions, inspections, comparisons and an awareness of progress which has been made, and that which remains to be made.

> *Quand j'étais petit, je n'étais pas grand.*
> *Je montrais mon cul à tous les passants.*

> When I was little, I was not a big guy.
> I showed my bottom to all passers-by.

This *formulette* is still heard all over France, and I have come across it in an almost identical form in a story attributed to the poet Étienne Pavillon and dated 1687.

It is true that the critic and the historian are not in the habit of studying children's games as a form of artistic expression, because they undertake their research with a certain preconception of poetry and literature. But if, for instance, we agree on the *convention* of

Marc Soriano

defining *poetry* as a *form* which has a sort of consistency and charm which make it stick in the mind and play a real role in the life of he who recites it, we cannot deny the poetic quality of the poem-game of *pince-sans-rire,* * which all French children know by heart, and which has made all of them laugh until they cried:

> *Je te tiens*
> *Tu me tiens*
> *Par la barbignette.*
> *Le premier qui rira*
> *Aura la clafette* (*la claquette*)
> (Version from La Creuse, *Ibid.*, p. 130)

> I have you,
> You have me
> By the chinny-chin-chin.
> And we'll give a smack (slap)
> To the first to grin.

In "riddle" games, the mixture of popular imagination and the sumptuous poetic imagery of its expression sometimes produces delicate lines reminiscent of Japanese haiku:

> *Qu'est-ce qui passe dans le bois*
> *Sans déchirer sa robe de soie?* — (Le soleil.)

> Who goes walking in the wood
> And never tears her silken hood? — (The sun.)

Because of their number, their quality and their variety, these *formulettes* rise like a veritable poetic continent whose exploration demands the concerted efforts of folklorists, linguists, historians, teachers, and so forth. At the present time, in this domain as well as

* *Translator's note*: literally: "pinch-without-laughing," a kind of staring contest. The word now implies dry humor in adults.

that of the fairy tale, research seems to have pushed aside the "problem of origins" in the somewhat rigid, formalistic nineteenth century sense of the phrase. Investigators accept the basically anonymous character and great age of the *formulettes*. All the scholars are in agreement on these two characteristics, although it is difficult to document them, at least for the moment.

Historians of language have no doubt been able to observe the traces of certain historic events in some of the *formulettes*. For instance, in the famous nursery rhyme *La Mère Michel*, one can find the story of Lustucru, one of the leaders of the "Barefoot Revolt" in Normandy during the first half of the seventeenth century, or in other songs collected by Bacaumont, references to the war of 1870 or to the Eiffel Tower. Other specialists, such as Marcelle Bouteillier, here and there have found traces of proverbs, witchcraft formulae, etc. It seems reasonable to believe, however, that these are not part of the original material, but are details added during one of the "updatings" and "revivals" which have insured the survival of these rhymes until the present time.

These observations would make it seem advisable to avoid the two extreme positions taken by certain specialists. Are the poems magical formulae, pieces borrowed by children from fragments of song, of sententiae, of fables, stories, etc., retained because of their sonority alone—that is, spontaneous creations by the children themselves—or are they conscious reworkings by adults? As Bacaumont says, these theories are not contradictory, but rather complementary. Their synthesis furnishes the most reasonable explanation of the origins of these children's rhymes, each of which nonetheless remains a special case which merits individual examination.

This rapid foray into a rarely traveled sector permits us to make a certain number of essential remarks on the evolution of children's literature. The experience of generations of simple people, of those natural experimenters—parents—discovered long ago, centuries before the educational psychologists, the pedagogical "trick" of associating the acquisition of indispensable knowledge with *games*. Even if it be only for this characteristic (and there are others) oral literature provides us with a veritable children's literature (or at any rate a perfectly differentiated current) at a time when this type of literature does not exist in the domain of the written, and when pedagogy has not recognized the child as a specialized audience. Popular tradition has produced these works through continual confrontation of the parent's educational intentions and the child's possibilities of comprehension and assimilation. Thus it has profited from the inventive power of the former and the fresh imagination of the latter. This parodoxical but natural collaboration has produced an incredible variety of methods and rhythms to which the examples I have given here cannot do justice.

The great quality of these nursery rhymes, in my opinion, is that artistic expression is never developed gratuitously, as amateurs of verbal games might tend to believe, but for its power of evocation and for its meaning. This explains their remarkable poetic value, which gives them a ritual value which both catches the child's attention, imbedding them in his memory, and astonishes the adult by their sobriety and richness:

> *Où est-il?*
> *Dans sa chemise, où il passe des deux bouts.*
> (Côte d'Or, *Ibid.*, p. 299)

> (Where is he?
> Inside his shirt, where he comes out at both ends.)

A certain number of not necessarily bad poets, for example Ratisbonne and Coppée in the nineteenth century, no doubt imagining that the French child did not have a poetic repertory comparable to the "nursery rhymes" of English children, tried to create one. This praiseworthy effort ended in failure. Certain critics have believed they could conclude from this that the "Frenchman does not have a poetic soul." I don't wish to be suspected of chauvinism, but I believe the failure can be explained in another way. Like all peoples, the French possess a literature for children which is both rich and varied. It is the very quality of this repertory which causes the almost automatic rejection of the greater part of poetry composed for children by "professionals." Our children are accustomed to a poetry of such astonishing fantasy, and moreover one so profoundly functional, that the indispensable task of rejuvenating their literature becomes extremely difficult, if not impossible. The Surrealists understood this: they alone have managed (and still it may be best to wait a little before making pronouncements) to furnish poems which children have accepted and assimilated, by using (Desnos in particular) the very procedures of popular poetry.

There is another important remark to be made. These rhymes are usually smiling or facetious, such as that of the agreement:

> *Entendu, conclu,*
> *Trente-six fesses font dix-huit culs.*
>   (Boulogne-sur-mer, *Ibid.*, p. 286

> O. K. Now we've got 'em
> Thirty-six buttocks make eighteen bottoms.

This elementary, basically scatological humor evidently reflects the uncensored style of life of the Old Régime, which gives it a simple, historical interest, but there is another trait which shouldn't be forgotten. Most of the products of this oral tradition make every effort to *teach children to laugh*. They admit frankly that humor, irony and gaiety are indispensable acquisitions for a child, because they permit him to dominate his problems and have faith in life. These are natural functions in each of us, but they need to be developed.

Let us not accept this orientation as the contribution of common sense. It is in reality an important experimental discovery, of a pedagogical method which literature for children of the future will need to reflect upon and draw inferences from. Laughter is not only "in

Marc Soriano

the nature of man," it is also a fundamental part of our adaptation to the world. We who are, who have been *made* to be sad adults, and who have more or less consented to this sadness, must try to have laughing children. Perhaps they will have more of a critical spirit than we, and that is truly indispensable if they are going to make our world a better one.

Translated by Julia Bloch Frey.

Marthe Robert

The Grimm Brothers *

In undertaking to collect, transcribe and publish the popular tales whose tradition was still alive in the German states at their time, the Grimm Brothers were scarcely thinking of more than preserving them from oblivion before their decline became irremediable. The extraordinary success of the two little books that rightly bear their name bespeaks sufficiently their success, which doubtless surpassed their hopes; for, thanks to them, their love and their scrupulous patience, these little masterpieces — once considered no more than tiresome stories — suddenly entered into the province of literature and even into the history of ideas. Indeed, before them, although Perrault had created a vogue for tales among persons of taste and letters, no one would have sought in tales anything other than the naïve, charming and rather simple products of a popular imagination of benefit almost exclusively to old women and children. If people amused themselves reading them — even writing them — they scarcely asked questions concerning the reason for their existence; and their meaning appeared clear enough to be summarized in a brief moral which combined the benefits of making them useful and of compensating for their oddities. It is probable that the German philologists themselves would not have gone far beyond this viewpoint if the logic of their method had not led them there by unexpectedly opening before them a path bristling with obstacles and questions. Their great merit is to have cleared this path in a country almost as thick with bushes as the enchanted forests of their tales, and to have taken the risk of following it.

Their admirable transcription was made with a fervor in which the piety of the ancient bard is no less evident than the exactitude

* Translation of "Les Frères Grimm," in *Sur le papier*, Editions Bernard Grasset, 1967. Printed with the permission of the publisher.

of the critic. On the one hand, it served poetry by restoring perfection and nobility to popular literature; but on the other hand, it provided the material for a true science, which had been inconceivable as long as there had been only a few isolated tales at hand, collected for fun or at random. As collections of the same type grew increasingly numerous and made European folklore better known, some extremely precise similarities were discovered among the tales, resemblances whose very constancy was such that it ruled out any explanation by fortuitous encounter. Indeed, not only did the narratives from highly diverse countries have a common plot, their elements were also identically arranged and combined, with the exception of a few variants — but these still underscored a clear continuity of the themes. How can such similarities be explained otherwise than by a common origin? But, once raised, the question of the origin and dissemination of the tales raised also the question of their possible meaning. For if these stories had passed from generation to generation, starting from a single origin, it was difficult to consider them as altogether absurd. On the contrary, it was necessary to believe that they had indeed had a meaning, which had naturally grown obscure as they moved ever further from their distant beginnings. In order to elucidate these problems, which caused the tales to lose their apparently harmless nature, the Grimm Brothers formulated an attractive theory which was long held to correspond to truth. In their capacity as philologists mainly preoccupied with the origins of their language, they were led to think that all the marvelous narratives forming the foundation of European folklore are of Aryan origin, and are to be regarded as more or less pale or vivid reflections of myths conceived in time immemorial by the race from whom the Hindus, the Persians, the Greeks, the Romans and most of the peoples of Europe are descended. As they moved about, the various Aryan tribes carried with them these remains of their mythology, which, with the variants and deformations produced by adaptation to new climates and to new forms of life, are encountered in all the tales of those peoples sprung from the same race. "Those elements," writes Wilhelm Grimm, "which we meet in all the tales are like the fragments of a shattered stone, scattered on the ground amid the flowers and the grass: only the most piercing eyes can discover them. Their meaning has long been lost, but it can still be felt and that is what gives the tale its value."

Hence the Grimm Brothers and the scientists of their school thought that they could explain the tales by the myths from which they are derived, reducing both to a single theory: for them, tales and myths are the representation of the great cosmic or meteorological drama which man, from the infancy of his history, has never wearied of imagining. Nothing was simpler, consequently, than to interpret, if not the details, at least the general outline of each tale: if the mythical characters are personifications of natural phenomena — stars, light, wind, tempests, storms, seasons — then Sleeping Beauty must be understood as spring or summer benumbed by winter, and the death-trance into which she is plunged for pricking her finger on the spindle-tip must be understood as the memory of the annihilation threatening the Aryan gods by the mere contact of a sharp object. It follows that the young prince who awakens her certainly represents the vernal sun. (Let us note that Perrault's version seems to support this view point: the Beauty and the Prince indeed have two children, Day and Dawn, whereas the German version stops at the marriage, as is usually the rule in tales of this type.) By applying the same reasoning process, we find that Cinderella is an Aurora eclipsed by clouds —the cinders of the hearth— which are finally dispersed by the rising sun, the young prince who marries her. And in every young girl who is exposed to the incestuous desires of her father and who covers herself with an animal skin to escape him (in the Grimm collection this is "Peau-de-Mille-Bêtes," a variant of Perrault's *Peau-d'Ane*), one must recognize Aurora being pursued by the blazing sun whose burn she fears. In this so-called "naturalistic" interpretation all the narratives have approximately the same meaning and the tale itself is pure metaphor; it is a poetic image, the veiled expression of a feeling for the world and nature such as the peoples of our countries conceived them in their childhood.

    We shall not enter into a discussion of a theory which was variously completed, extended, or refuted and which has today no more than an historical value. Let us take note, however, that it was destroyed above all by an acquaintance with non-European folklore. This new knowledge was to throw into relief the kinship of all tales regardless of their origin. At one and the same time too narrow and too broad, the Grimm Brothers' theory appears today as an hypothesis; but to it we owe a fruitful juxtaposition of two orders of phenomena formerly very far apart in scholars' ways of thinking. By endeavoring to establish the relations between the tale and the myth, this theory brought out for the first time the universal human experience which the tale, as well as the myth and the legend, is charged simultaneously with veiling and transmitting. And that is what counts much more than the translation into plain language of the fairy-world allegories; for this experience is at the root of every supernatural narrative: it may have taken different forms but it did not cease to assert itself in spite of the greatest social and religious changes. Hence the fairy tales which spread into countries long since Christianized restore to us with surprising fidelity a number of rites, practices and customs which reveal a tenacious attachment to paganism. And these are not simple residual memories, for the tale, as has long been observed, has something to teach: it is, in its modest fashion, a small didactic piece. What indeed does it express beneath its fantastic coloration? Essentially it describes a passage — a passage which is necessary, difficult, hampered by a thousand obstacles, preceded by apparently insurmountable trials, but one which ends happily in spite of everything. From the most improbable fabulations a very real fact always emerges: the necessity for the individual to pass from one state to another, from one age to another, and to be formed through painful metamorphoses which terminate only with his accession to true maturity. In the archaic conception which lives on in the tale, this passing from childhood to adolescence, then to manhood, is a perilous ordeal which cannot be surmounted without a previous initiation; that is why the child or young man in the tale, having gone astray one day in an impenetrable forest with no visible way out, meets at the right moment a wise person, generally old, whose advice helps him out of his bewilderment.

If the French tradition weakens the initiatory nature of the tale in favor of an ill-disguised eroticism and a generally conformist morality, the German tale, manifestly less "civilized," preserves it in all its strength. The difference is very perceptible when the two traditions treat the same subject — Cinderella, Sleeping Beauty, Peau-d'Ane — especially concerning the central character, the fairy. It would be useless to search in the majority of the German tales for a fairy in a sparkling dress, with a star on her forehead and a wand in her hand, who arrives in the nick of time to arrange love-matters for young people. She is replaced by a character who bears scant resemblance to her and whose unobtrusive personality is in striking contrast with the fairy's splendor. Most frequently it is an old woman whom the narrator does not bother to describe but whose appearance does not fail to be ambiguous; for at first sight one does not know exactly what to expect from her: is she a tutelary power or a witch bent on doing evil? This disturbing old woman is altogether deprived of radiance, arousing no admiration, no gratitude, no love. Gaunt and emaciated even when promoting happiness, she in no way recalls the radiant fairy who for the orphans merges with the tender figure of their lost mother. The old woman appears seldom; she is encountered when the hero is lost with no recourse left. She is not the "godmother" of those whom she assists: if occasionally she is present at their birth, she does not attend their wedding; and as soon as her task is done, she disappears. In short, she is so little endowed with the traits indispensable to the fairy that it is almost tempting to refuse her this quality.

Actually, the German tale does not generally call her "fairy"; when she is given a name, it is that of "wise old woman," what in French we would call a *sage femme,* a term we may well want to keep precisely because of its double meaning of "wise woman" and "midwife," and because of the interpretation of which it admits. As a matter of fact, before being a sorceress or a witch, the *sage femme*, like the Greek Fates and the Germanic Nornes, seems indeed to preside over the birth of man, whose destiny she represents. (It will be noted that the old woman in our stories is often a spinner.) But if we confine ourselves to popular language, which makes a midwife of the *sage femme*, we can suppose that in archaic society, where her image became fixed, the fairy is one who brings children into the world and enforces the rules of *sagesse*, that is, who supervises the strict observance of the rites presiding at childbirth and at every important act of life. Although her characteristics have been considerably downgraded, the old woman in Grimm's tales has partially retained her role as guardian of rites and tradition, a fact which explains the awe and respect which usually surround her. Neither good nor bad, neither fairy nor sorceress, she is one or the other as the case may be in order to remind us of the necessity for those ritual customs which give meaning to life's important events. In *Sleeping Beauty*, for example, Grimm tells us that in her father's kingdom, there are in all thirteen *sages femmes* (Perrault mentions only seven fairies, but the last one is excluded from the birth ceremony for a similar reason). Now the king cannot invite them all because he owns only twelve golden plates — and obviously, the *sages femmes* cannot be served out of any other dishes. The thirteenth is thus "forgotten" and this oversight, this breach of ceremony, produces as a consequence a serious interdiction for the child: that of using a spindle, that is of carrying out the occupations of a young girl in a normal manner. This interdiction leads to a new oversight, for all the spindles are destroyed except one, left in the hands of an old woman in whom we might well recognize the *sage femme* herself. There follows a final trial, an attenuation of primitive death: the sleep of a hundred years, which the correct accomplishment of the nuptial rite will alone bring to an end. Ill born, since her birth is accompanied by the omission of an act, the Beauty cannot develop without risking death at every moment. Her passage into adolescence is effected while she is in a deep trance, and it is only after a long delay that she awakens at last to love.

The Grimm Brothers

Midwife, woman full of knowledge, and, of course, sorceress thanks to her close relation with the obscure forces of life, the *sage femme* informs us better than the romantic fairy of our country about the task with which her model of ancient times was probably charged: to transmit to those individuals whose need is greatest — children and adolescents — a knowledge of the religious and social practices by which man can fit himself into the order of things, can truly come into the world and find his place. If such is her function, one can at last understand the paradox of the tale which, at all times intended for children, gives preferential treatment to the subject the least appropriate to children's literature: the erotic quest for the beloved through a thousand painful trials. In reality, the contradiction exists only for us, according to the criteria of our pedagogical morality: the character of the *sage femme,* trustee of rites, initiator and counselor in the true sense of the word, easily allows us to dismiss this paradox. Consequently it can be seen why the tale is at once so innocent and so cruel, why it takes pleasure in evoking bloody acts, murders, mutilations, human sacrifices, as if it were a question not of revolting deeds but of things to be taken for granted. This is because cruelty is closely bound to the ritual world of which the tale is the distant reflection; and far from having to cover up the gory side of life, the tale is there, to an extent, to make it manifest. It is not surprising that the supernatural narrative flows with blood; that maidens maim their feet at the moment of their marriage (for example, Cinderella's two sisters exposed by the "blood in the slipper"), or have their hands cut off by their fathers (*The Girl without Hands*); or that fathers sacrifice their sons (*Faithful John, The Twelve Brothers, The Raven* and many more) and husbands their beloved wives: the shedding of blood consecrates the ritual passage which none can escape. The bloody sacrifice may also be accomplished by asceticism: total fasting, prohibition from speaking and laughing (often accepted by maidens for the salvation of their brothers), long periods of isolation in the forest. In any case, the trial justifies the existence of the tale, the very substance of its teaching. It may be wondered how this teaching was maintained in

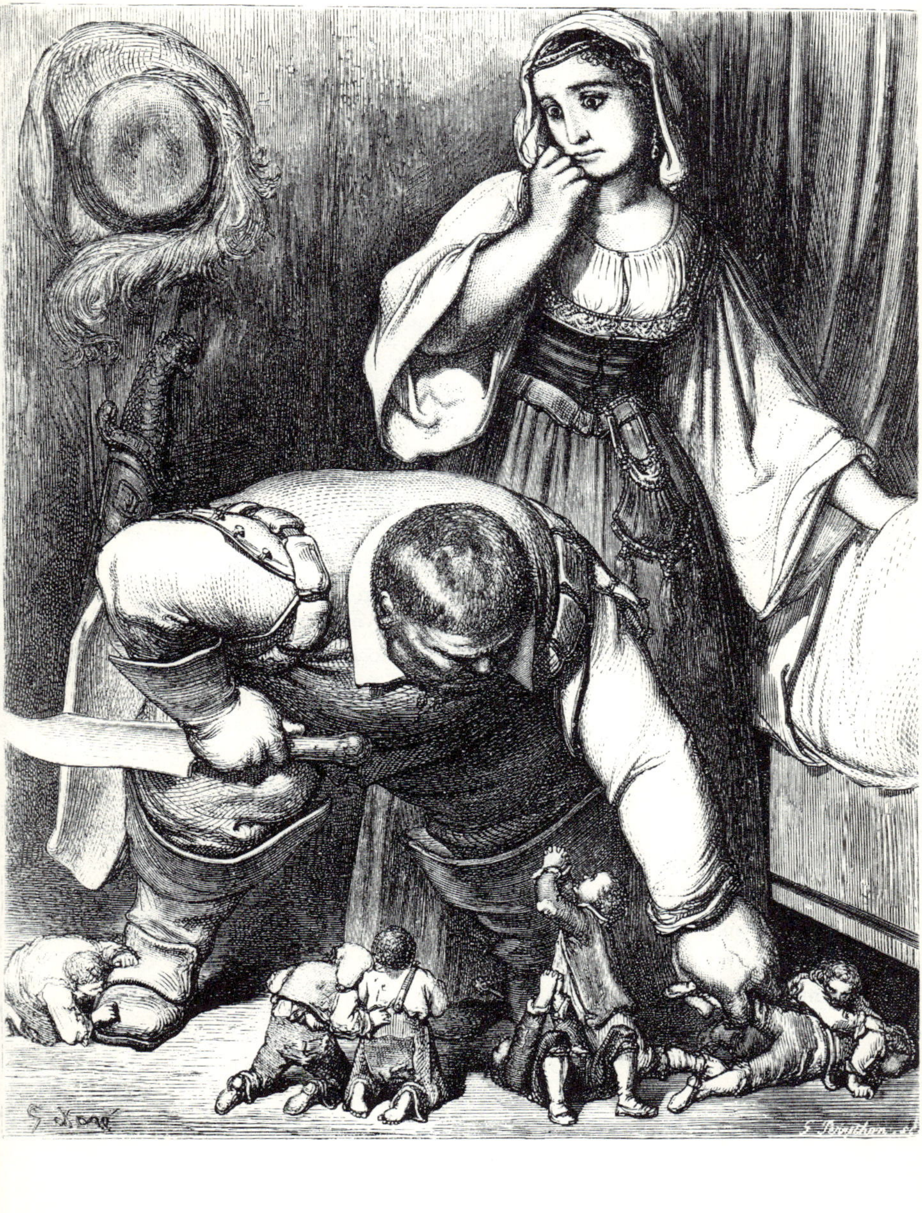

the presence of so many obstacles, in spite of the powerful currents tending to abolish it, and especially in spite of Christianity. Perhaps the tale owes the continuation of its teaching to these old women — good-natured souls or nurses — who, sitting by the hearth, transmitted it from generation to generation, and who modestly played (probably without knowing it) the formerly prestigious role of the *sage femme* and the fairy.

It is apparent that the most obvious qualities of the tale — its ingenuousness, its childish charm — are far from justifying its surprising survival. In reality, it is deeply ambiguous; and if the simplicity of its design is pleasing, it fascinates us with all the truth that can be sensed in it, even if we do not attempt to interpret its truth. However masked it may be by symbols and images, it nevertheless speaks a more direct language than the myth or fable, for example; and children know this instinctively, "believing" in it insofar as they find in it what interests them most of all: an identifiable image of themselves, of their family, of their parents. Doubtless, that is one of the secrets of the tale, and the explanation of its endurance: it speaks solely of the human family, it moves exclusively in that restricted universe which, for man, long emerges with the world itself, and sometimes even replaces it altogether. The "kingdom" of the tale is indeed nothing else but the universe of the family, closed and clearly defined, in which the first drama of man is played out. There is no reason to doubt that the king of this kingdom is a husband and a father, and nothing else; at any rate, it is thus that he is presented to us. It may be assumed that his fabulous wealth and power and the extent of his possessions are present merely to throw the paternal authority into relief; for as far as the rest is concerned, it has to be admitted that we know nothing about him. Most of the time the tale simply introduces him with the traditional formula "Once upon a time there was a king," then immediately adds "who had a son..." The king is at once forgotten as the tale focusses on the adventures of the son, until the end, when the king is remembered solely for the final reconciliation. It is exactly the same when the king is replaced by an ordinary man, which, as will be seen in many a tale of the Grimm collection, produces no appreciable change in the story. Whatever symbolic value one may assign him, the king — at least in what we see of him — is simply a man defined by his physical and emotional ties with the members of his family. He is never a bachelor; and when he is a widower, as he frequently happens to be, his most pressing business is to remarry (again the affairs of state are mentioned here only in order to enhance his power, for the ordinary man acts no differently. "When winter arrived," says the narrator of *Cinderella,* "the snow placed a white carpet on the tomb; and when the springtime sun had removed it, the man took another wife"). The king cannot remain without a wife, even less without children; and if he should happen to find himself in such an awkward situation, the tale hastens to extricate him. The queen, for her part, has no other function and no other reason for being than that of wife and mother. As for the prince and princess, they are pre-eminently son and daughter, at least until such time as, establishing a family of their own, they cease to be interesting.

With a surprising art of abridgment, the tale (and especially those of Grimm) thus presents us a little family novel whose outline is, as it were, invariable: a child is born into an anonymous family in a non-specified place (the anonymity of the location is constant, but it will be observed also how rarely the characters' names are mentioned in our stories: the hero is simply spoken of as the "prince" or, more often, as the "young man"); he is, as the case may be, either loved by his parents or mistreated by them; and it is noteworthy that the worst treatment comes especially from his mother, whose ferocity strongly contrasts with the somewhat cowardly (and somewhat amusing) kindness of the father. (In the Grimm collection only two or three wicked fathers are to be found, such as in *The Goose Girl at the Well* and in *The Twelve Brothers*; whereas the cruel stepmothers can scarcely be counted. And the fact that this unnatural woman is presented as a stepmother cannot deceive us as to her true nature: it is indeed a question of the cruel, devouring, jealous mother. For the tender, loving mother devoted to her children is, with few exceptions, always a person far away or the memory of a dead woman.) The childhood of the supernatural hero is never without accidents: if he is loved by his parents, he is hated by a brother or a sister. If he is surrounded with affection, he is pursued by an offense committed prior to his birth, generally by one of his family: an oversight, a rash vow, a naïve promise made to the devil. Hence he cannot grow up normally: he hardly reaches adolescence before he must leave his family and go out, according to the hallowed formula, to seek his fortune "in the wide, wide world." There, in this perilous world where he inevitably loses his way, he is exposed to poverty, the anguish of loneliness, the first assault of love. Then he must set out on a road strewn with pitfalls, pursued by an evil willpower, as if distance itself could not take him away from the fatality of the family. His only chance of salvation is to meet the beloved being who will "deliver" him from the enchantment in which his childhood attachments still hold him. Woe unto him if he cannot sever them with a firm hand, and forever: by cutting off all the dragon's heads with their tongues, for example. If, yielding to the nostalgia which propels him towards his birthplace, he forgets the prediction of the maiden whom he loves and embraces his parents "on the left cheek" or says "more than three words" to them, that is enough to plunge him back into oblivion, unconsciousness, or the chaos of childhood which he has had so much difficulty leaving. And if, day dreaming, he accepts a wife from his parents, renouncing his own free choice, he loses himself for a long time by losing his "true fiancée."

True, the fairy-tale prince should not, without further precautions, be equated with Oedipus, for the reason that the tale never treats the theme of incest from his point of view, but always from that of the father, whose desires are often very crudely revealed (the theme is less submerged in the numerous stories in which fraternal love predominates). But everything suggests that the danger which the prince is fleeing in leaving his family is the very one spoken of by the ancient tragedy. The only difference is that he always triumphs over the trial and is spared Oedipus' double crime: however violent the conflict played out within the theatre of the kingdom may become, the prince has the strength to surmount it; however tenacious his childhood attachments may be, he is enabled to break them and to "live happily ever after." As an example of a perfect success precisely in the area where Oedipus fails, he brilliantly demonstrates, in the course of a highly condensed dramatic action, that the metamorphosis of child into adult is full of perils but possible, and that this alone can lead man to that high degree of happiness in love which the tale makes its human ideal.

With its epic characteristics and style, the fairy tale is thus still a true novella of "sentimental education"; and probably nothing better justifies its pedagogical vocation. Its purpose is serious beneath the appearance assumed for giving amusement; and there is nothing to prevent us from thinking that it is aware of its responsibility. But what grace it has as it exercises the function it chose for itself! What art it puts into its manner of instructing! And how well it chooses its details, with what liberty, what humor — in spite of its own conventions — it shuffles the cards of reality and dream, truth and illusion. Although it is concerned only with the kingdom of desire, where nothing separates a wish from the fulfillment thereof, it looks at everyday reality — the reality of obscure labor, of the suffering and compulsory patience of each day — with lively, clairvoyant, gay or sad eyes, but always full of warmth and shining with a love for life. If it proposes a consoling world in which all misery is compensated for by the realization of the most impossible desires, it has too much respect to make misery itself vanish. On the contrary, it mournfully shows the wounds misery makes. To be sure, the fairy tale abolishes natural laws just as it pleases; but it remains well in contact with flesh and blood, it never overlooks the body of its hero. It describes him as he falls a prey to poverty, hunger, cold, the harsh fatigue of the road. The tale recalls even the misfortunes of war; always before elevating the simple soldier to the status of royalty, as he deserves (if not by his virtue by his valor and trials), it first shows him discouraged and humiliated, bitter and ready for anything, just as one finds unemployed mercenaries in all ages. The tale does not merely give life to the vast domains whose all-powerful king is the dream; like every profound and poetic work, it is attentive and respectful of life in its most humble manifestations. It earns thereby its principal privilege, which is that of lying without accrediting illusion, while remaining true.

Grace and art — that is what, in the final analysis, the tale can find in itself as its strongest protection against any disquieting undertakings that may come from science. No one knew it better than the Grimm Brothers, whose first concern was to preserve the tales, as it were, from their own temptations as researchers, seeing to it that nothing impure adulterated them, even if it were to enhance or enrich them. It is by a miracle that they succeeded in this, or rather by the effect of a rare alliance between scholarship and poetry. Like the child of their last tale, they hold out to us the golden key which they think they have found beneath the snow; but they do not force us to take it. The key is so beautiful, of such fine workmanship and of such pure splendor, that we can be content to admire it, without thinking of putting it to use.

Translated by Wyley L. Powell.

Isabelle Jan

Children's literature and bourgeois society in France since 1860

When country children used to listen in the evenings to their grandmothers telling the story of *Cinderella* or *Tom Thumb,* the cultivated public attached scant importance to these tales. Perrault, seeing the pleasure which children found in them, was the first to measure their possibilities and to suggest the desirability of using them for pedagogical purposes: "People of taste have noticed that these trifles were not mere trifles, that they contained a useful moral, and that the playful narrative surrounding them had been chosen only in order to fix the stories more pleasantly in the mind and in such a fashion as to instruct and amuse at the same time . . . Is it not praiseworthy of parents, when their children are not yet capable of appreciating solid truths stripped of all charm, to make them love these truths and, as it were, to make them swallow them by enveloping them in pleasing narratives suited to the weakness of the children's age?" [1] This intuition had no consequences. In any case, Perrault could not truly appreciate the meaning and the social and ethical import of the fairy-tale hero. He could imagine even less the use which family morality would later make of the children's book.

Indeed, the hero in the fairy tale appears with certain demands, although, to be sure, he does not openly oppose society upon discovering his state of dependency. Even less does he strive to remedy it in any positive way. But he does keep a distance between himself and the arbitrary; he rejects the weight of a certain fatality; and finally he compensates, circuitously and symbolically, for the misfortunes of destiny. Hence, the one who does not resemble the others, who is detached from the mass by the chance of birth or the absurdity of

[1] Charles Perrault, Preface to the fourth edition of the *Contes en vers,* 1695.

circumstances, the one who is weak in body, dull in mind, or obscure in origin — Tom Thumb, Simple Simon, the *Heimatlos* — is also the one to whom we are drawn and who, as the situation is reversed point by point during the story, becomes the strongest or the cleverest. Wandering and homeless, he conquers a kingdom. In short, in the fairy tale the pariah is the hero.

Children's literature of the eighteenth century, and even more so that of the nineteenth, while it derives its inspiration to an extent from folklore (though less than one might think, particularly in France), does not continue this comforting vision of power relationships among individuals. Children's books of the eighteenth and first half of the nineteenth centuries were intended to be edifying. Their clearly-stated goal was to educate the child according to the dictates of good behavior as instituted by a rising, voracious bourgeoisie, nostalgic for aristocracy and forgetful of the common people from which it had sprung. This is evident if one consults the mass of works produced between 1780 and 1830 by such educators as Mme de Genlis, Berquin, Mme Cottin, Bouilly, Julie Gouraud, etc. [2] Throughout this purely "demonstrative" literature, the child appears as a cog in the immense social machinery. His conduct is always considered in terms of the adult world, which wishes to develop in him, depending on the social rank to which he is promised, either the qualities of the leader — courage, endurance, authority, self-control — or those of the servant — docility, gentleness, gratitude. Of course, the didactic purpose is foremost and is so apparent that it prevents all possibility of dramatization. No ambiguity, not the slightest questioning is to be found in these playlets and anecdotes. Frozen in their roles, provided with all the attributes of these roles, the characters are entirely positive. They unite all their efforts toward the successful outcome of a scientific experiment: to prove that everything is to be gained through good behavior and all to be lost otherwise. Nothing of this enormous hodge-podge has survived, which is as it should be; for this was

---

[2] Paul Hazard has given a remarkable analysis of this literature in his *Les Livres, les enfants et les hommes* (Flammarion, 1932).

Isabelle Jan

what we would call today propaganda material, without the slightest transposition, and in no wise a literary phenomenon.

Children's literature in France began to develop in the second half of the nineteenth century: starting in 1860, to be exact, when the desire to edify, as contrasted with that of entertaining, moved into the background. This occurred thanks to the stabilization in power of the bourgeoisie and to the expansion of education, factors which produced a larger book-reading public of children eager for knowledge. A certain liberalism in education then introduced the notion of leisure and of profitable leisure, and culture thus became one of the means for the ruling class to form its élite and consolidate its ascendancy. And, as a result, publishing made great progress, with production costs becoming lower and, at the same time, the printing and copying processes becoming simpler and more widespread. This increased freedom given to inspiration, and this new flexibility in the instrument itself, favored the blossoming of original talent. One writer in particular, the Comtesse de Ségur, was responsible in France for revivifying this literature, without, however, breaking with its conventions.

With Mme de Ségur the moral is indeed identical to that found in Berquin, but it is only one element of the story and, as such, is integrated into it; there it plays its role, which may then become interesting and, frequently, ambiguous. With her all activity proceeds from the real and tends to reproduce it and imitate it. In the first place, there is play, play which transforms, though it does not invent, and which always needs a concrete prop: a toy or a simple utensil taken from everyday life. On the other hand, all activity, whether ludic or not, which departs from the real introduces a disturbance and unbalances the edifice. And the real is here, of course, the social order: a rigorous organization which holds together owing to a skillful regimentation which everyone must promote. The decrees of Providence, the logic of circumstances and events, and the good will of men are associated in the common effort so that each person will be justly punished or rewarded and the rich will be charitable and the poor grateful. Otherwise, corrective measures must be introduced.

Events take care of that, but sometimes these are simulacra of events, that is (once again) play. Certain social disparities, while scandalous in themselves, do not deserve the wrath of heaven. The wicked rich are generally punished, but they may also be made fun of and, in that way, put in their place. It is obviously ridiculous to see grocers giving a fashionable soirée, and so we see it disturbed by the pranks of the painter Abel.[3] A family of parvenus, the Tourne-Boules, mimic the aristocracy; they are aped in turn by the children, and so normal order is restored.[4] Adults and children are accomplices in this undertaking of rearrangement. It is therein that the role and importance of Mme de Ségur's anti-heroes can be verified. Indeed, everything takes place as if certain children, the real heroes — "model" boys and girls — were endowed by the adults with some of their power. In the case of these children, all acts, whether ludic or not, assume a meaning and are given an organization within the social circle, tending to maintain order and to bring a new stone to the edifice. Other children, on the contrary, born troublemakers, move about in vain outside the circle, unable to gain admission. Mme de Ségur demonstrates her superiority to the fabricators who preceded her in the supple and varied manner in which she presents these disturbers, the glimpses which she provides us concerning their profound motivations and the complexity of their relationships with the other characters. There is a chasm of difference between the behavior of a child who is ill-bred as a result of being too spoiled, such as Georges in *Après la pluie le beau temps*, and that of the ill-bred child who has been too often beaten, such as Sophie Fichini; between an unfortunate rebellious lad like Jean-qui-grogne ("Grumbling John") and a pre-adolescent girl quick to take offense like Félicie in *Diloy le chemineau*. Their only point in common is that they all are situated outside the norm. Endeavouring to bring these exiles into the norm is a task to which the positive characters dedicate themselves with a passion so insistent and excessive that it seems to us complex, often contradictory, and weighty with implications.

[3] *Jean qui grogne et Jean qui rit.*
[4] *Les Vacances.*

Isabelle Jan

All of this, which should be given a close analysis, confers a special tone to the works of the Countess and makes reading of them fascinating even today.

Yet this children's literature, at the same time that it was developing a satisfactory mode of expression likely to attract an original talent, was also accentuating its status as a literature reserved for one class. One can better grasp the social import of this by comparing such children's literature with the popular nineteenth-century *feuilleton,* or serial-novel, with which parallels have often been drawn. In this regard the *feuilleton* indeed demonstrates greater subtlety, if only in the relationship between author and public. If children's literature was produced, in a simple direct circuit, by bourgeois writers — established men of letters, society ladies, schoolmarms and other teachers — for the children of the bourgeois, popular literature, likewise composed by authors more accustomed to Parisian salons than to the low social strata they described, pretended nevertheless to address itself to a public which, if not altogether of the people, was at any rate modest and unassuming. And this differentiation is indicated in the very nature of the means of financing and diffusion. The newspapers [5] in which the novels of Eugène Sue appeared — or those of Balzac, Alexandre Dumas, and other less prestigious writers — were read backstairs and in garrets, whereas children's newspapers remained a luxury until the founding of *L'Épatant* in 1907. Furthermore, the majority of children's literature went to its public in the form of the book, the beautifully produced volumes of the Hetzel Collection or Hachette's *Bibliothèque rose.* It is therefore not surprising that the serial-novel remained closer to the compensatory archetypes of the folk tale, with its rebellious heroes and disguised princes. To consider only the children characters, it is in books for adults that silhouettes appear recalling the fairy-tale heroes: strange, wild creatures like the children of George Sand, disgraced beings like Tortillard (whose name means "deformed cripple") in *Les Mystères de Paris* — all of them rejected, solitary, lost, and more or less execrated individuals. These young characters, pitiable, comical, or

---

[5] For example, *La Presse* of Emile de Girardin.

disquieting, whose twisted features stick in the reader's memory, are really isolated creatures who never meet their socialized counterparts, as they do in Mme de Ségur. They are mistreated, humiliated, defeated, to be sure, but free and consequently ready to dare the perils of adventure. Tortillard, Petite Fadette, Cosette, Gwynplaine (the child disfigured by the *comprachicos*), and later, Jacques Vingtras, Jacqou le Croquant ("Clod-hopper"), and Poil de Carotte ("Carrot Top") — not one of these figures in the children's books. The only free, adventurous, non-socialized children at the beginning of children's literature in France are the young heroes of Louis Desnoyers: Jean-Paul Choppart and the extravagant Robert-Robert. But are we not here precisely halfway between popular and children's literature? Can it be said that the novels of Desnoyers are intentionally written for children?

When popular literature became a weapon of combat, when it was incarnated in the works of Hugo, Michelet, Vallès, it provided the explanation for the disgrace of these children. The child becomes a deformed solitary being and reaches this stage of "atrophy," to use Hugo's word, because he is a victim of society. When the English manufacturers complained to Pitt that they were being ruined by the excessive wages that they were paying their workers and that this was preventing them from paying taxes, he replied: "Then take the children!" The exploitation of children, that crime at the outset of the Industrial Revolution, was denounced in France by various investigations, in particular by those of Villermé (*Tableau de l'état physique et moral des ouvriers des manufactures de coton,* 1840) and of Léon Faucher (*Le Travail des enfants à Paris,* 1844). Literature for its part, while echoing this situation, rarely embodied it in flesh-and-blood characters but rather expressed it symbolically. Michelet was one of the first to see in the child an image of the oppressed and innocent People: "The child is the interpreter of the People. Nay, he *is* the People with their inborn truth before they become deformed, the People without vulgarity, without uncouthness, without envy, inspiring neither distrust nor repulsion. Not only does the child interpret the People, he also justifies and exonerates them in many

Isabelle Jan

things. ... No, childhood is not merely an age or a degree in life, it is the People, the innocent People."[6] And that is how the figure of Gavroche appears to us. Gavroche is exemplary in that, more so and better than any other personage in *Les Misérables,* he represents the purity of the proletariat. However, he also represents, and in no less exemplary a fashion, the encounter of childhood with events. Few authors have been capable of that or have dared to emphasize it, as if childhood were in itself a protection, as if it interposed a screen between the individual and unstable reality, which remains a vague background and does not directly influence the destiny of the young hero. At best, events serve as a pretext. The Alsatian children of *Le Tour de France par deux enfants,* by Bruno, would not have accomplished their journey and beheld so many wonders if they had not been driven out of their province by the defeat of 1870. But the child-hero, swept along by circumstances, tossed about by social or national upheavals, remains passive. He does not participate in the confrontations of the adult world. And yet he could take part in it — and in quite a specific way. That is what perhaps a sole French novelist understood: Erckmann-Chatrian, in reality two Alsatians — Émile Erckmann and Alexandre Chatrian — yet so closely united in their common work that it is permissible to speak of them in the singular. In several of his *Romans nationaux et populaires,* and we have in mind especially the admirable *Madame Thérèse,* Erckmann-Chatrian placed the child in a precise historical context, but also in the place that is naturally his, that of an observer: an observer who is attentive and intelligent, but naïve also and frequently absent-minded, solicited from all sides, and not always by what seems to us the essential thing — but for that very reason unattached and open to all possibilities. Hence, the events — in this instance the campaigns of the Year II (by the Republican Calendar) and the Battle of Phalsbourg — are seen through the eyes of a child. Through his terror, his perplexity, his questions, his enthusiasms, the disorders are explained and truth comes to light. Then the child truly becomes "the interpreter of the people." But it is significant that Erckmann-Cha-

---

[6] Michelet, *Le Peuple,* Part II, chapter IV.

trian is considered by academic and literary critics, and by the public itself, to be a third-rate author. France remains unaware that this master story-teller, as attentive to the presence of beings and things as to the necessary progression of the narrative, this writer whose sensibilities were so profoundly attuned to popular aspirations, was in reality her Dickens.

Going from so-called "popular" literature to children's literature, one notices that this double theme — the child of the people and the child faced with events — almost completely disappears, except in some precise and acute notations of the Comtesse de Ségur [7] and in certain pages of Hector Malot. [8] Behind this lies a manifest desire for silence, but one that is masked under various pretenses. The destitution of children is evoked by means of conventional, hence reassuring, characters: the orphan, the child of wealthy background fallen into financial ruin and now a "little poor boy," the circus boy (often the son of a bourgeois kidnapped by gypsies), and especially the little boy who is ill: so many aliases, so many alibis concealing from the bourgeois public the true character, who would be entirely too disagreeable and disturbing. On the contrary, children's literature in France endeavored to integrate the child into the social world by presenting it to him in a comforting fashion, that is by sanctifying his environment: the family, the school; by ennobling such concepts as work and the fatherland. One can gain quite a complete view of this idealism by leafing through the pages of the *Magasin d'Éducation et de Récréation,* published from 1864 to 1915 by Jules Hetzel and Jean Macé. It represents perfectly the state of mind of those responsible for education, and of the artists who took an interest in this particular means of expression. For all the illustrators and children's authors of the period collaborated on the *Magasin,* with the exception of Mme de Ségur, who is definitely a special case: "Among all these works ... there is not a one ... which will not bring its share to the series and which will not furnish its young readers, instead of a

---

[7] Cf. Pierre Bleton, *La Vie sociale sous le Second Empire, un étonnant témoignage de la Comtesse de Ségur* (Paris: Les Éditions ouvrières, 1963).
[8] In *Sans Famille,* the mine episode; in *En Famille,* the life of the girls working in the northern spinning mills.

Isabelle Jan

sterile pastime, substantial material for good and useful reflections. All the shortcomings, large and small, to which youth is subject are ingeniously and delicately combatted therein; all of youth's good inclinations are lovingly encouraged. Writers and artists ... have obviously agreed to offer nothing to the mind and eye which will not vouchsafe the child moral benefits and, at the same time, entertainment; and if, as it is said, 'a good work is that which most resembles a good action,' none of their works can be better than these." [9] And it must be recognized that, on first sight, the authors submissively conformed to this program. To begin with, the children in these stories are seen to be absolutely protected by the constant and efficacious presence of their family. There are no unworthy parents in the *Magasin d'Éducation et de Récréation,* no harsh blows or bad treatment; fewer parents still who are negligent or frivolous, as they are in Mme de Ségur, or even fallen from their position, as it sometimes happens in Anglo-Saxon authors. On the contrary, the parental function is of a heightened value. Fathers and mothers represent not only a tender, protective refuge but also a mentor, and every word that they utter must be taken as definitive. The examples are innumerable, and a particularly enlightening fact is that Hetzel-Stahl signed his books intended for the youngest children as "a Papa." He was a Papa to whom the draftsman Froelich gave the physical appearance of a good-natured Jupiter (the actual appearance of Hetzel, moreover) accentuated still more by the majesty of the beard sported at that time by men of the bourgeoisie.

To this unquestionable omnipotence of the family unit must be added the authority of the school. The schoolmaster is a double of the father, and teaching begins in the home. The child is already prepared upon entering school to receive submissively the words of the *Magister*: as Hetzel himself well expresses it: "We shall thus continue to accord great importance to instruction, especially to that part of instruction which cannot be included in the programs of public schooling and must be the preserve of the family. Our role is to complement, but not duplicate, the instruction given at the public

[9] Introduction to the *Magasin d'Éducation et de Récréation* by the Comte de Grammont, Year 1864-65, second semester, p. 224.

and private schools. The intelligent teachers and attentive schoolmistresses who have often been so good as to write to us realize that the aid which we might give them would in no way conflict with their teaching, which must keep its unity." [10] The first consequence of this symbiotic relationship between instruction in the family and instruction in the schools is a presentation of the latter as a magic place. It would be tedious to point out the obsession in these texts with the "good pupil" — the idea that, outside of the school, there can be no salvation, and that only the school leads to the highest destiny. Let us take note, however, that this hallowing of education, which replaced the cult of high birth, leads to the formation of a type of individual who offers nothing new, in whom is firmly maintained the hierarchy of the three social orders: the learned man, that is the scholar; the soldier; and the manual worker. Hence, the ideal proposed to the child is that of becoming an engineer, a teacher, an administrator, an officer. And it is quite natural to find, beyond this social segregation, a hierarchy of professions. If indeed the manual worker is represented, it can be only as a peasant or an artisan. It is fitting to instill into the child a feeling for the nobility of work; such an awareness can be acquired only by direct, individual contact with the material involved. The farmer obeying the rhythm of the seasons, or the artisan fashioning an object from beginning to end, can put love into his work. The lowly laborer in the workshop or at the bottom of a mine, carrying out some obscure, fragmentary job, would have been unworthy of representing the working-class and of expressing the joy of work well done; hence, these lowly workers are absent from children's books. Like little Francinet, the hero for whom another book by Bruno is named, the child reader was to understand that "work is as good as prayer," and that he could, along with the hero, strike up the "song of the poor":

>   From cradle to grave
>   Long is the chain of my labor!

---

[10] "A nos abonnés," Introduction to *Magasin d'Éducation et de Récréation,* Year 1864-65, second semester, p. 375.

Isabelle Jan

> But work makes the heart proud,
> Idleness makes for cowardly hearts.

And, to emphasize further this process, great effort was made to divert from the child's mind any association between the notions of work and profit. This idea, so frequently voiced, finds a particularly characteristic expression in a novel by Gennevraye, *Marchand d'allumettes*:

"So, sergeant, you thought you'd find the most amusing job in the service?"

"In the first place, lad, it's not a job but a profession."

"What's the difference between a job and a profession?"

"Oh! What difference...? What difference...!" The sergeant kept looking for his words, but without success. Then his face brightened. "A job, Zidore, is what earns you money; a profession is what earns you honor: such is the military profession." [11]

This ethic takes on a particularly caricatural aspect in the books of *Sélections* used by the schools. In them the idea of duty, or *devoir* (it must not be forgotten that schoolwork is called *un devoir* in French) ushers in a tone of sadness (sometimes going so far as sadism) which prevails throughout. Let us listen again to Michelet: "People refuse to see in childhood anything other than an apprenticeship for life, a preparation to living, and most children are not living at all. They can be happy "later," people say; and, to assure the happiness of those uncertain years to come, children are overwhelmed with boredom and suffering, thereby being deprived of the one short moment of which they can be sure ... I am not speaking of the crushing burden of the work nor of the innumerable and excessive punishments that we inflict on their mobility, given them by Nature herself. I am speaking rather of the inept harshness which leads us to plunge a young being abruptly and imprudently into cold abstrac-

---

[11] *Magasin d'Éducation et de Récréation,* Year 1888-89, first semester, p. 108.

tions, a child still warm, scarcely severed from the mother's blood and milk, and who asks no more than to burst into bloom." [12]

The image of society emerging from these texts can only paralyze the child and turn him away from any initiative that may lie outside of the beaten path. Since there is no way out, the ground becomes favorable for the crystallization of myths: honor, heroism of the humble... It is indeed better to consider that there is something heroic, even romantic, in doing what others want you to do, when there is nothing else that you can do. What other ambition can one have than to enter this society and become a respected, if not truly active, member of it by embracing a liberal career? In this manner, aspirations for change are averted, and the very notion of adventure is effaced.

More exactly, there is a fusion of duty and adventure. France under the Second Empire and the Third Republic, launched by Louis-Napoléon Bonaparte on senseless military ventures; then, after the defeat of 1870, haunted by the idea of revenge, and involved furthermore in the machinery of the colonial wars, this France possessed specific objectives to propose to the energies of her children: thus adventure entered into the service of nationalism. And one can understood why Louis Veuillot and even Monseigneur Dupanloup [13] extended their felicitations to the editor of the *Magasin d'Éducation et de Récréation*, a publication founded by republicans, men hostile to the régime of Napoléon III, unconditional partisans of secular education, like Jean Macé, which published popular novelists like Erckmann-Chatrian and even *Communards* like Elisée Reclus and Paschal Grousset. [14] This is striking evidence that the nineteenth-century writers of children's books, irrespective of their political persuasions, remained both ethically and aesthetically conservative.

Are we then once more in the presence of an impoverished expression subjugated to the necessities of indoctrination, stifled by

---

[12] *Le Peuple,* Part II, chap. IV.
[13] Cf. A Parménie and C. Bonnier de la Chapelle, *Histoire d'un éditeur et de ses auteurs* (Paris: Albin-Michel, 1953), page 489 ff.
[14] Who used the name André Laurie when signing his works for young people; they were concerned with school-life in various countries.

conformity and by the sterility of a good conscience, devoid of openings, disquiet, and imagination? One would be tempted to believe that such was the case were there not, rising from the midst of this wearisome twaddle — and much in evidence in the pages of the *Magasin* itself — the name of Jules Verne. Without going into a searching analysis of Jules Verne's thought and the subconscious motivations of his work, [15] it would nevertheless be interesting to see here how, having set out from certain highly influential ideas — those of a complacently expansionist society which had perverted for its own profit the high ideals of its forefathers — he was able, at one and the same time, to dramatize these ideas and free himself from them in order to do creative work. Thus, without questioning the profound harmony and fraternal feelings which prevailed between Verne and Hetzel, it is certain that at the base of this mutual comprehension there was a sort of misunderstanding. Hetzel expected to use Verne for didactic purposes and, ostensibly, Verne carried out these intentions. But ostensibly only; for in a way which was no doubt obscure but which becomes clear to us today, the meaning hidden in Verne's work is quite different. His power over the imagination, which has only increased in a century, is the best proof of it. Hetzel wanted to have Verne write the scientific novel, that is, he wished to bring modern knowledge within the reach of young minds. Stated differently, it was an attempt at popularization of knowledge akin to that which he proposed to Viollet-le-Duc (*Comment bâtir une maison?*), to Jean Macé (*Les Serviteurs de l'estomac*), or to the naturalists from whom he solicited amusing studies on the life of insects, animal societies, etc... In this way, geography, geology, and astronomy — in relation to the great world explorations, preludes to the colonial wars — devolved upon Verne. Verne could thus, as the opportunity presented itself, assume the role of ethnologist and point out the presence on every continent of the white man, of the civilized Occidental manifesting everywhere the supremacy of his intelligence, of his knowledge, of his energy and drive.

[15] Cf. in this regard the remarkable work of Marcel Moré, *Le très curieux Jules Verne* (Paris: Gallimard, 1960).

To be sure, all of that is in Jules Verne, especially in his early novels, from *Cinq semaines en ballon* to *L'Ile mystérieuse*; but, in so doing, on another front, Verne attacked — no doubt without realizing it himself — those very values which Hetzel wanted him to defend when he imposed this program upon him. Defender and propagator in the domain of knowledge, Verne was to become an innovator in literature. And it is in this respect that his work was to survive, because it broke with a whole literary tradition. In the first place, he quite simply made this break by *writing* for children. Of course, that meant instructing and therefore molding them; but Verne wished to do so while remaining fully a writer and an artist. In his writings the didactic intention comes only in second place. Now, on the artistic side, creating for children at that time was itself an innovation. (This prejudice is still extant in France.) But in a more profound sense, one that touches the essence of the novelist's art, Verne was one of the first to abandon psychology, to forsake the idea that a novel is first and foremost a piece of psychological analysis. Hetzel was aware of this; basically, he never completely believed in the genius of his author, or did not recognize wherein it actually lay. Consequently, he laments to Verne in countless letters over the weakness or improbability of his characters. In fact, Verne was in the process of transforming the very object of literature. He was not one to introduce parcels of knowledge into the framework of human adventures treated in conventional terms. Tradition required that the characters should exhibit those virtues which were to be instilled into the young, and that obstacles and difficulties should be discussed in terms reminiscent of Corneille. To read Verne in this way, as Hetzel would doubtless have liked, is not to read him at all. In his case, it was not a question of making science attractive, but of making science itself the object of literature. In other words, he was experimenting with a new aesthetics of the novel, the same that Poe had inaugurated; and in so doing, Verne's work was revolutionary. But if Verne had shown himself to be an innovator, if he had made an opening and introduced imagination into children's literature—imagination as a defense against social conditioning, and

Isabelle Jan

as a means of going beyond the fundamental elements immediately proposed or imposed — his work was at once to be misinterpreted, stifled, or misapplied. In this sense, the case of Verne may be taken as symbolic of the reactions of the cultivated French public toward a phenomenon that it neither foresaw nor controlled. To begin with, there was a total failure to appreciate his talents: silence settled about the artist. Verne's name figures in practically no history of French literature. Then he was abruptly discovered. When, in the wake of curious and ingenious readers such as Marcel Brion, Marcel Moré, or Michel Butor, it was realized that Jules Verne was one of the great visionaries of the nineteenth century, he was snatched, as it were, from the children, to be handed over to a public of initiates. The French critic has difficulty in admitting that children's literature can be the bearer of poetry. And, unfortunately, the books written for children, from Verne to the present, seem to justify that view. To be sure, there were a few works from 1925 to 1940: realistic novels like those of Charles Vildrac or Colette Vivier; creations of pure fantasy, such as the tales of Marcel Aymé; debatable and unconvincing works examining the world of childhood, such as *Le Petit Prince* by Antoine de Saint-Exupéry, or, more essential and better developed, the fantasy by Maurice Maeterlinck, *L'Oiseau bleu*. But the balance-sheet indicates relative poverty; and the works taken as a whole are lacking in continuity and vigor. The possibilities, at once liberating and subversive, of a dialogue between the child and himself, such as *The Wind in the Willows* or *Winnie-the-Pooh* offer him; or the possibilities of a will to emancipation, as in Mark Twain; or again, of an objective view of social reality; and especially the perennial capacity of humor and fantasy to go beyond the exterior reality of things for the sake of an exploration whose consequences are unforeseeable—these possibilities have been so timidly realized in France that one can virtually conclude that they remain virgin territory. This can naturally be explained by the excessive regimentation of children. In France, probably more than in any other industrially developed country, the organic link between family and school was, until quite recently, absolute, both defending the same values and holding the same conceptions of work and culture. For more than a century the French elementary and secondary schools, a monolithic block into which any innovations creep at a dishearteningly slow pace, have seemed to be totally in harmony with the aspirations of an omnipresent middle class whose progressive spread should not conceal its essentially static nature and which, in the final analysis, represents only itself. An organized circuit connects the schools with certain sectors of the publishing industry, which, in addition to textbooks, provide collections of recreational reading that continue the learning process; with the theatre, which illustrates the authors of the "syllabus"; and with the literary critics, who deliberately ignore the deep-seated needs of individuals under sixteen and patiently await the pupils' arrival at that age to bring them into contact with their own authoritarian conception of a certain function of literature. Every form of expression not satisfying their criteria is condemned either to vegetate or to be co-opted by new mechanisms of inflationist and repetitive commercial production.

The upheavals that have just taken place in the schools will surely have, sooner or later, an influence on this form of expression. Until the present time, and with few exceptions, children's literature was only a tool in the hands of families and educators dispensing the morality of the well-behaved child and the model schoolboy; now it has become a simple consumers' product. Tomorrow it will perhaps be able at last to offer children a vision in which they will recognize themselves not as adults would like them to be but as they really are, in action and freedom.

Translated by Wyley L. Powell.

Esther S. Kanipe

Hetzel and the Bibliothèque d'Éducation et de Récréation

> But, regardless of author, I adored the works in the Hetzel series, little theatres whose red cover with gold tassels represented the curtain; the gilt edges were the footlights. I owe to those magic boxes —and not to the balanced sentences of Chateaubriand— my first encounters with Beauty. When I opened them, I forgot about everything. Was that reading? No, but it was death by ecstasy. *

By 1870, the central position of the family in French society was accepted by the society's critics as well as its supporters. Anarchists totally condemned it, while conservatives, such as Msgr. Freppel, the bishop of Angers and deputy to the National Assembly from Brest, defended it as "an incomparable element for fixity, stability, permanence, and cohesion." [1] In *Centuries of Childhood,* [2] Philippe Ariès shows that the modern family, in which a couple and their children form the basic unit, developed among the bourgeoisie after the sixteenth century. This development was complemented by a new attitude towards the child, who was recognized to have a character and needs different from the adult, and by the designation of childhood as a distinct period to be devoted to an education which would

---

* Jean-Paul Sartre, *The Words,* trans. Bernard Frechtman (New York: George Braziller, 1964), p. 73.

[1] As quoted in Jacques Desforges, "La Loi Naquet," in *Le Renouveau des idées sur la famille,* ed. Robert Prigent, Institut national d'Études démographiques, cahier no. 18 (Paris: PUF, 1954), p. 108.

[2] Trans. Robert Baldick (New York: Vintage, 1962).

prepare the child for adulthood. The responsibility for guiding the child to adulthood was assigned to the family, whose biological and legal functions were now supplemented with moral and spiritual obligations. The child's importance within the family increased until, by 1880, Paul Brotier, Director of the École Normale of Parthenay, could declare, "It can be said without exaggeration that today the child plays the leading role in family life." [3]

The Franco-Prussian War brought invasion, defeat, and civil war to France. After the rude shock of defeat, the nation turned to its youth as the hope for the future, and the child became a subject for serious concern, not only in the individual family, but in the society at large. The nation's educational structure was a topic of wide political controversy during the Third Republic, and underwent profound changes such as the establishment of free compulsory laic primary education. [4] The social sciences, which were just beginning to emerge as separate disciplines, focused attention on the child in order to determine how individuals and societies developed. The child appeared as a major figure in adult literature, while the literature written for the child experienced a vigorous and creative expansion. Leading philosophers, scientists, politicians, artists, and publishers, such as Pierre-Jules Hetzel who edited the highly esteemed "Bibliothèque d'Éducation et de Récréation," now recognized the formation and education of France's children as the critical task of their generation.

Pierre-Jules Hetzel (1814-1886) began his publishing career in the 1830's, and soon became a leading figure of the Parisian literary world. Among the important works which he published were Balzac's *La Comédie humaine,* several of Victor Hugo's later books, and much of the writing of Georges Sand, to whom he was also a close friend and advisor. In addition to his publishing activities, he enjoyed considerable success as a writer, beginning with the satirical *Scènes de la vie publique at privée des animaux* (1842), and was actively involved

---

[3] "L'Enfant," *Revue pédagogique,* VI (octobre, 1880), 484.
[4] Antoine Prost, *L'Enseignement en France 1800-1967* (Paris: Armand Colin, 1968).

Esther S. Kanipe

in the politics of the July Monarchy through his association with the republican newspaper *le National*. He served in the Provisional Government of the Second Republic as Lamartine's *chef de cabinet,* and supported General Cavaignac for the Presidency. Because of his political activities, he was forced to live in exile in Belgium during the Second Empire. Before his exile, he had been totally immersed in the considerations of his own generation, but, under the impact of 1870, his concern shifted to the next generation. In January, 1871, he wrote to his son:

> Our poor France! well, the unhappier she is, the more we love her, and better! It is our generation which has let her fall into this abyss; it is yours, my child, which will pull her out of it. And force will not be the first weapon to seize. No, no. It is by uniting education and training that this misguided country must be returned to her path. That, first of all. Did we lack rifles, did we lack hands? No, it is science... and, above all, discipline... We must rebuild among our people the respect for the good and the beautiful, respect for right and law, respect for superior quality: in a word, *respect*. The nation of scoffers created by the empire has collapsed. God grant that none are left. It the lesson did not cure us, then we might as well say "finis Galliae"! If we learn from it, it is the opposite of death, it is resurrection. [5]

From 1870 until his death, children's literature became Hetzel's primary interest. While still in exile, he had established, in collaboration with his childhood friend Jean Macé, [6] the Bibliothèque d'Édu-

---

[5] A. Parménie and C. Bonnier de la Chapelle, *Histoire d'un Éditeur et de ses auteurs, P.-J. Hetzel (Stahl)* (Paris: Éditions Albin Michel, 1953), p. 536.
[6] Jean Macé (1815-1894) was a teacher at the Lycée Henri IV in Paris. In 1866, he founded the *Ligue de l'Enseignement* for the encouragement of education, and, in 1883, was elected to the Senate where he was involved in the reorganization of primary education. Among the most successful of his many works of children's literature was *Histoire d'une bouchée de pain* (1861), a child's explanation of physiology.

cation et de Récréation, which published children's books and the *Magasin d'Éducation et de Récréation* (1864-1915), an encyclopedic bi-monthly magazine. In pursuit of his aim simultaneously to amuse and educate, he sought authors from all disciplines. He secured contributions from historians, scientists, popular novelists such as Hector Malot and Jules Verne, poets such as Victor de Laprade, educators, and even an architect, Viollet-le-Duc.[7] Hetzel and the authors associated with him presented the reader with a specifically committed view of the problems and possibilities of French society.

The bourgeoisie was the dominant element in the society which appeared in the Bibliothèque. Heroes were either middle or upper class, and stories which dealt with family life portrayed bourgeois families. A few servants were pictured sympathetically, but always in subordinate roles. Major characters were never of working class origin, and the occasional working class character was presented in one-dimensional terms; pets were much more warm and alive on these pages than were working class people. The peasantry were praised for their traditional virtues of honesty, perseverance, and patriotism, but were rarely of any real importance as individuals.

The geographical setting of the story was always described in detail, and had a significant influence on the action. Though the authors of the Bibliothèque gave little attention to the peasants, they spent a considerable amount of time extolling the advantages of the countryside over the city. Hector Malot's dislike of the city was particularly obvious, as in his novel *Sans Famille,* where all of the hero's unhappy experiences occur in cities, especially Paris, while

---

[7] Hector-Henri Malot (1830-1907), the son of a government functionary, studied law, but soon turned to literature and became a successful journalist and novelist. His most popular works included *Sans Famille* (1878), *Roman Kalbris* (1869), and *En Famille* (1893). Jules Verne began to publish with Hetzel in 1862 with *Cinq semaines en ballon,* and was the most popular author of the Bibliothèque. Pierre-Marin-Victor Richard de Laprade (1812-1883) was a professor and poet who considered himself a disciple of Lamartine. In 1858, he was admitted to l'Académie française. He published many collections of poetry, including *Le Livre d'un père* (1876), and several prose works on the history of literature. Eugène-Emmanuel Viollet-le-Duc, architect and art historian, wrote, among other works for children, *Histoire d'une Maison* (1873).

he finds relief and help when he reaches the countryside. When a peasant is forced to work in Paris, he returns to the country a cruel and greedy man. Malot described Paris as "These wretched houses, these sheds, these dirty courtyards, these vacant lots where piles of refuse rise — this was Paris." [8] Hetzel also preferred the countryside: "I much prefer the places that are not talked about at all, that the stranger does not visit, that are left alone, which keep their refuges and secrets, their flowers and sentiments, their hard troubles and simple pleasures." [9]

The Bibliothèque was not intended to convey an idealized image of the world. Hetzel's goal was to present reality, or what he felt was reality, and to prepare the child to deal with it. He sought to create an awareness of the problems which he saw in society, and to guide the child toward becoming the person who could solve them. He interpreted the nation's real difficulty as derived from the attitudes of the populace, and envisioned positive change through education. The emphasis fell always on what the individual should do with his life, what virtues he should practice, for the solutions to France's problems lay in the creation of the good citizen.

To be part of society, it was necessary first to be part of a family; those without families were always outsiders in a very restricted social world. The plight of the child who must live without a family was the central concern of the genre of "l'enfance malheureuse," of which Malot's *Sans Famille* is an example. Rémi, the hero of *Sans Famille*, wanders about France as an itinerant musician, and, through his eyes, the reader sees that the orphan has no place in French society. Malot's presentation was realistic:

> In the village there were two children called "the children of the alms-house"; they had a numbered lead plate about their necks; they were dirty and poorly dressed; they were mocked and beaten; the other children often chased them as

---

[8] *En Famille*, Vol. VII of *Œuvres choisies* (Paris: Fayard, 1898), pp. 12-13.
[9] *Maroussia*, as serialized in *Magasin d'Éducation et de Récréation*, XXVII (1878), 23.

one chases a lost dog for amusement and also because a lost dog has no one to defend him. [10]

Even more terrible is the description of Garofoli who has twenty orphans who work for him as beggars and street musicians. They are poorly fed and housed, and beaten often; Garofoli is finally imprisoned when he beats one boy to death. Although Malot recognized the cruelty of this situation, he did not present it as a problem which the society should attempt to solve. Rémi's suffering ends when he is reunited with his family, and assumes the position in society which is his birthright. For Malot, the ideal was always the family, and the orphan's life was merely an ordeal through which the hero must struggle to find his proper place in society. If families held together, the problem would disappear. He never concerned himself with all those orphans whom Rémi had encountered in circumstances far worse than his own, and who never found their families.

Whatever the society's problems, religion was not expected to solve them, for the religious element is almost entirely absent from the society that appears in the Bibliothèque. Characters never go to mass and priests rarely appear and never play a major role. The existence of organized religion is totally ignored. Characters may give token recognition to the will or grace of God, but God never actively intervenes in their lives, and they seem to expect nothing from Him. If deliverance is necessary, it most often comes through scientists or scientific knowledge, as it does in Verne's *L'Ile mystérieuse;* the characters calmly apply their knowledge to the situation at hand and save themselves. *Sans Famille* contains a striking condemnation of the folly of religious differences and quarrels. Among a group of men trapped in a coal mine are a Calvinist and a devout Catholic. The two argue, each accusing the other of some terrible sin which brought disaster on them all. One man confesses that he has stolen money, is ostracized by the group, and commits suicide. The author repeatedly switches the scene between the men in the mine and the efforts of an

---

[10] *Sans Famille,* Vol. VI of *Œuvres choisies,* p. 23.

engineer who is calmly and scientifically working to help the trapped men. They are saved by science, not by religion.

The crucial position of science in this literature is exemplified by the fact that the first article of the first issue of the *Magasin* was "Les Serviteurs de l'Estomac" by Jean Macé. This emphasis on science was continued by articles such as "Promenade d'une fillette autour d'un laboratoire," "Histoire d'une population d'insectes," and "Histoire d'un Hôtel de Ville et d'une Cathédrale." The aim, approached primarily through the transmission of concrete factual information on either technical subjects or nature study, rather than any abstract scientific principles, was to inspire admiration and respect for science. In the course of adventure stories, the plot was often deserted for pages for a recitation of something which the author considered valuable knowledge. In *Un Capitaine de quinze ans,* Verne used a character interested in natural science to introduce a three-page explanation of the scientific classification of the animal kingdom, especially insects. These attitudes towards "nature" and "science" can perhaps best be illustrated by this quote from an article entitled "Les Mystères du monde des mites": "Nature—what an admirable book! What inexhaustible riches, what a variety of subjects for study it offers to the man who knows how to apply his mind to it and turn the pages with patience and contemplation! What discoveries one can yet make here with the aid of the new means at the disposal of science!" [11]

The bourgeois child reading the authors of the Bibliothèque confronted a reflection of his own society in which some nostalgia for a simpler time was mixed with hope for the future through science. The imperfect world would present each individual with problems, but the correct attitudes and actions could solve them. The reader was urged to base his decisions on the methodology of science instead of on religion. The heroic character illustrated what actions would be the best for the individual and for France.

Although he was not xenophobic and expressed no sense of any inherent superiority through being French, Hetzel's aim was patriotic.

---

[11] *Magasin*, XXVII (1878), 114.

He was attempting to inspire a rebirth of the pride and spirit which he felt had been lost during the Second Empire. The heroine of *Maroussia* clearly reveals this intention. She is a young Ukrainian girl vho sacrifices her life while trying to help free her country from the Russian invaders. Although war is not portrayed as all glory and patriotism and the enemy appear as human beings, not as ogres, the "Jacobin" sense of the citizen army defending *la patrie* is praised. The author's awareness of the contemporary parallel is obvious: Maroussia is "a young Joan of Arc... Happy the nations, small or large, who have the right to sing their 'Gloria victis'!" He concluded his novel: "There is unhappily more than one Ukraine in the world; God grant that, in all the countries that have been forced to submit to the foreigner's yoke, there will be born many Maroussias, capable of living and dying like the little Maroussia whose story we have just told." [12] Any doubt as to his intentions is erased in a letter to a friend: "Do you know what gave me the courage to do this work? I said to myself that our Alsatians and Lorrains would be able to dream of a future analogy with their own situation, to draw from it the love of an insurrection at *the right moment*." [13]

The most praised characteristic of every hero is his self-control. As he indicated in his letter to his son, Hetzel considered discipline the most important corollary of science. Maroussia is calm and in control of herself, even though she is ten years old and surrounded by a company of enemy soldiers. Total self-possession is the key characteristic of every Verne hero. The Spartan virtues are praised in the story of a child who faces death "very much the master of himself." The necessity for discipline on a less serious level is treated with equal sobriety in a story aimed at teaching the importance of punctuality because "a man has a position, social obligations, his life to make; what is the first condition for any professional success? punctuality..." The child must exercise this control to make himself work hard:

---

[12] *Maroussia*, p. 54; p. 378.
[13] Parménie and Bonnier de la Chapelle, p. 602.

"That child who understands from the beginning that work is the law of life... is probably predestined for great things."[14]

The hero acts alone. The individual nature of his actions is emphasized by the absence of any involvement in groups. Groups rarely appear and, when they do, individuals within the group possess no identity outside it; the group is never presented in human terms. There is occasionally a friendship relationship between peers, but this is an individual-to-individual arrangement. If there is a relationship based on affection, outside the family, it is usually with some animal. The heroic figure never feels any identity with a group. Groups, other than the family and the nation, are simply not considered a significant enough aspect of a person's life to be worthy of attention.

It is the family which is charged with the creation of this disciplined, patriotic, scientific individual. The need of the child for the family is stressed continually, as in a short story about a small girl who insists on doing everything for herself. When she runs away from her maid while taking a walk, she is lost, and is returned home only when she accepts help from a kind stranger. Her mother uses this experience to try to teach her that she can never survive alone: "At age five as at ten, at fifty as at twenty, one needs his parents."[15] Children are urged to appreciate and obey their families through the story of a young hen who rebels against parental authority and is sold to a strange farm, where she realizes what she has lost.

Despite the confidence which Hetzel placed in the family, he recognized that it might fail in its educational role. In 1878, he wrote on this subject for the *Magasin,* though such articles addressed to elders were extremely rare in this publication. His basic message could be summarized as "Women, do not spoil your children." The article was an expression of a real concern that women, especially grandmothers, were not teaching their children self-discipline. He also urged

---

[14] All of the above examples, plus a great many more, are found in a single volume (XXVII) of the *Magasin*. The frequency with which the child was bombarded with this admonition to self-discipline makes it even more significant.
[15] F. Dupin de Saint-André, "Moi, toute seule," *Magasin,* XXVII (1878), 3.

children to understand that "by asking their parents to depart from the rules, by drawing parental tenderness to the point of weakness, they are working against themselves."[16] In his novel *Un Pot de crème pour deux,* he reaffirmed this point by the story of a small boy who became an undisciplined brat whom no one could like because his grandmother indulged his every whim.

A survey of the relationship between the hero and the family, however, reveals a curious ambivalence in these writers' attitudes. Family life, with the child at its center, is portrayed in these works, but no child ever commits any heroic action *within* the familial situation. The stories dealing with family life are always either a matter of the child doing something wrong, and the wise parent disciplining him, or of the parent spoiling the child, resulting in grief for the child. Heroes, on the other hand, either perform their heroic acts outside the family or else have no family, although they may dream of having one, and many novels end with the orphan's being adopted or discovering that he has a family somewhere.

Thus, the typical hero as described in Hetzel's "Bibliothèque" emerges as a person in complete control of himself, capable of great self-discipline. He is motivated by patriotism; his approach to life is scientific. He longs to be part of a family, and that may be his reward at the end of his adventures. Paradoxically, he has grown up without a family, yet is the epitome of all the virtues which the family should teach. The family is presented as an instrument of control and education where the parent must master his feelings for the child in order to teach the child to master himself. The hero acts as an individual; groups, other than the family and the nation, have no place.

Pierre-Jules Hetzel considered himself a liberal and a republican, a rational man, an admirer of modern science. He began to publish children's literature as a good businessman, and as an editor concerned with high standards of craftsmanship for his editions; his ideal was to fight "against the ugly and vulgar book, and against the poorly printed and poorly illustrated book." [17] After 1870, childrens' literature

[16] "La Morale est une," *Magasin,* p. 83.
[17] Marie-Thérèse Latzarus, *La Littérature enfantine en France dans la seconde moitié du dix-neuvième siècle* (Paris: PUF, 1924), p. 155.

represented much more to him: it was the channel to future generations, and these generations were the hope of France.

He and his associates summarized a world view and an ethic which the Third Republic wished to fix in the collective consciousness of its children. "Discipline and science, the two levers which can raise the world." [18] If this love of discipline created a generation which would support and protect the Republic, which would not permit 1870's disaster to recur, it also created a force for the perpetuation of the status quo. The ideal of the French bourgeoisie was the middle way where extremes were to be avoided. Actions and reactions could not overstep certain bounds, or they might upset the balance of what Stanley Hoffman has called "the stalemate society." [19] Children were a volatile force and could exercise a great variety of emotions. The ethic of discipline, if instilled early enough, could force this spirit into the necessary activity of protecting the status quo. The family served to both promote and control this energy. The children were simultaneously a hope and threat.

This conflict, between the encouragement of heroic individualism and the attempt to subordinate the individual to the control of the family, was inevitable in a view of society where relations between human beings were conceived only in terms of a struggle, and where the concept of a heroic group was unacceptable. Despite the presence of an obvious patriotic motive, even the army was presented as a group of individuals united momentarily to accomplish something necessary for the nation, and not as a distinctive unit with *esprit de corps*. The only collective idea to which the individual was expected to give his allegiance was the abstract entity of *la patrie*. This ethic was a deterrent to collectivities such as classes and religions whose differences might endanger the nation and upset the society's balance.

The family served as an instrument to insure that individualism itself did not become a dividing force; the individual who had not passed through the family's education in discipline was plainly

---

[18] "Une conférence de M. Jean Macé au Cercle pédagogique de Nantes," *Revue pédagogique*, IV (juin, 1884), 556.
[19] "Paradoxes of the French Political Community," *In Search of France* (New York: Harper Torchbooks, 1963), p. 3.

excluded from society. The child was made vividly aware that his acceptance into society depended on the existence of his family. L. Dugas, writing at the turn of the century, described his first and strongest memory from childhood:

> The only thing of which I am sure is that the idea of the orphan, rather the vague terror caused by this badly understood idea, enters me, stupefies me, overwhelms me, fills me with a sentiment of ill-defined sadness. It is this sentiment which commands all my memories, which evokes them, which makes them rise, groups them, specifies them. [20]

In *Saint Genet,* Sartre presents, through the life and work of one man, the interaction and conflict among these concepts of the individual, the family, the ethic of discipline, and the society. Genet is the being whom Hetzel's society most feared: the individual who has not been subjected to the family's discipline and control. Genet is unable to have any reciprocal relationship with another person, and feels absolutely no sense of himself as part of any collectivity; his life is "solitude carried to the point of Passion." Yet, Genet so totally accepts the values by which the society has rejected him as evil that he makes of his life as pure an expression of Evil as he possibly can. If he can never have a place in the society, it is because "Being nobody's son, he is nothing." Thus, "I know intuitively, by the simple contrast between his blundering haste and the slow, sure movements of the decent people about him, that he is a déclassé, an incompetent who has never been able, or never wanted, to submit to any discipline." [21]

---

[20] "Mes Souvenirs affectifs d'enfant," *Revue Philosophique,* LXVIII (novembre, 1909), 506.
[21] Trans. Bernard Frechtman (New York: Mentor Books, 1963), p. 664; p. 67; p. 51.

Marion Durand

One hundred years of illustrations in French children's books

To speak of image and illustration in French children's books from 1860 to the present is to note a gradual impoverishment, on the one hand technical degeneration, on the other an incredible loss of imagination — two factors which are of course linked.

In 1864, Pierre-Jules Hetzel (with Jean Macé) founded the *Magasin d'Éducation et de Récréation,* which appeared twice a month until 1915. Hetzel surrounded himself with carefully chosen collaborators, and he himself, under the pseudonym of P. J. Stahl, wrote works designed for very young children: books about "Mademoiselle Lili's Day," "Mademoiselle Lili the Housewife," "Little Sisters and Little Mothers," etc.

Lorentz Froelich's illustrations accompanying the Stahl texts are at the same time sensitive and strong. The artist knew how to give children life without making them cute. Froelich's children are never pretty in angelic fashion: they are solid little beings, stocky, well-muscled, who are not disguised like dolls in a shop window; they seem comfortable, in easy and anodyne clothes, as they go about the various activities of their daily life.

What is most noticible in these sketches is the seriousness of gesture: each action has weight, the character is completely absorbed by what he is doing, all of which reveals great intuition, a good psychological knowledge of what activity represents for children: a taking possession of the real, multiple apprenticeships, the learning of equilibrium and corporeal independence, so many essential factors which make us feel the growth of the child.

Froelich represents games as a serious, intense but calm activity. It is significant that the pictures showing a child playing abstract the background. You can see the child playing with his toy (doll, tea-set, donkey-cart) but nothing around him: the surrounding framework has been effaced, the rest of the world no longer exists and all attention is concentrated on the play activity and its meaning.

The second essential element to note in the pictures of Froelich, one which explains the feeling of security which emerges from them, is that one finds in them a permanent dialogue. The child is always represented in a relationship: the character always finds an interlocutor — another child, an adult, an animal, a toy. When it happens that the child is presented alone, he is turned toward an invisible person, outside the picture's frame, listening to him or speaking to him.

The child characters of Froelich, caught in their simple daily activities (playing, learning to put on their shoes, washing, eating, sleeping) are also located within the framework of their daily life. The albums of Stahl and Froelich show distinct categories of children; the difference in social rank is clearly visible: Mademoiselle Lili is a wealthy little bourgeoise while little Marie is the child of poor peasants. The difference in class is never underlined; each one has her family, her home; the children are shown to be different without being compared. Modern books no longer have the courage to represent social differences; however it would be wrong to assume that this children's literature of the nineteenth century was revolutionary. The poor child is shown as happy; and no one lifts his voice against inequality. The ideology which underlies these pictures is that of a universal happiness founded on an immutable social order. These pictures valorize familial tenderness and the joy of activity, where each person, of course, stays in his place.

The *Magasin d'Éducation et de Récréation* series did not publish only works designed for small children. The essential part of its publications was addressed to older readers; the picture was conceived of as an illustration for a much larger text. All the works of Jules Verne appeared in this collection, with illustrations by Bayard and Neuville, Riou, Meyer, Bennett, and others.

La Jangada appeared in 1881 with illustrations by Bennet which seem very characteristic of the genre. Certainly the text of *La Jan-*

LILI A COURU RETROUVER SA BONNE POUR FAIRE RÉPARER
LE DÉSORDRE DE SA TOILETTE

gada, like all Verne's stories of travel and adventure, is particularly suited to elicit illustrations which are on the frontier of the fantastic. Bennett's engravings are usually pictures with a recession in depth: one must enter the landscape, pass beyond a threshold, beyond which is another deep and mysterious world. Several constants are worthy of note: almost all the pictures are constructed around a nucleus of light. Since the density of the obscurity virtually smothers certain parts of the picture, the light areas appear so much the more luminous. There are sometimes two islands of light which respond to each other, and which balance the whole of the picture. It would be difficult to find an exclusively vegetable or mineral landscape in Bennett's engravings; each picture encloses a swarming of life, animal or human, hidden in a blossoming vegetable universe where the branches and leaves are twisted and coiled, and lose themselves in the depths of obscurity. In addition to the light, the frequency of subterranean or dormant water, of closed forms, of animals such as the serpent or the bird, seem to be elements of a symbolism at once obvious and complex. These images, compact and somber at first glance, call for an analytical vision; you don't perceive the whole, you don't receive a total image, you rather discover its elements little by little, and organize them as the eye becomes accustomed to the darkness. It is a process analogous to that of nocturnal vision; forms emerge from the shadows when the eye, adjusting to the night, rediscovers new possibilities of perception.

It is certain that children like the engravings of Doré, Riou, and Bennett. Such graphic and complex lyricism does not disorient them; it furnishes rather a support for the imagination. The visual imagination of these pictures nourishes the sensibility of the child; in a word they are pictures that dreams are made on.

One must remember that the Surrealists particularly liked the engravings of this period. It has been maintained that the young Rimbaud wrote "Le Bateau ivre" after having read *Twenty Thousand Leagues Under the Sea,* the text of which is accompanied by surprising and brilliant illustrations by Riou. It is rare today to see illustrations which do not present an obstacle to the imagination,

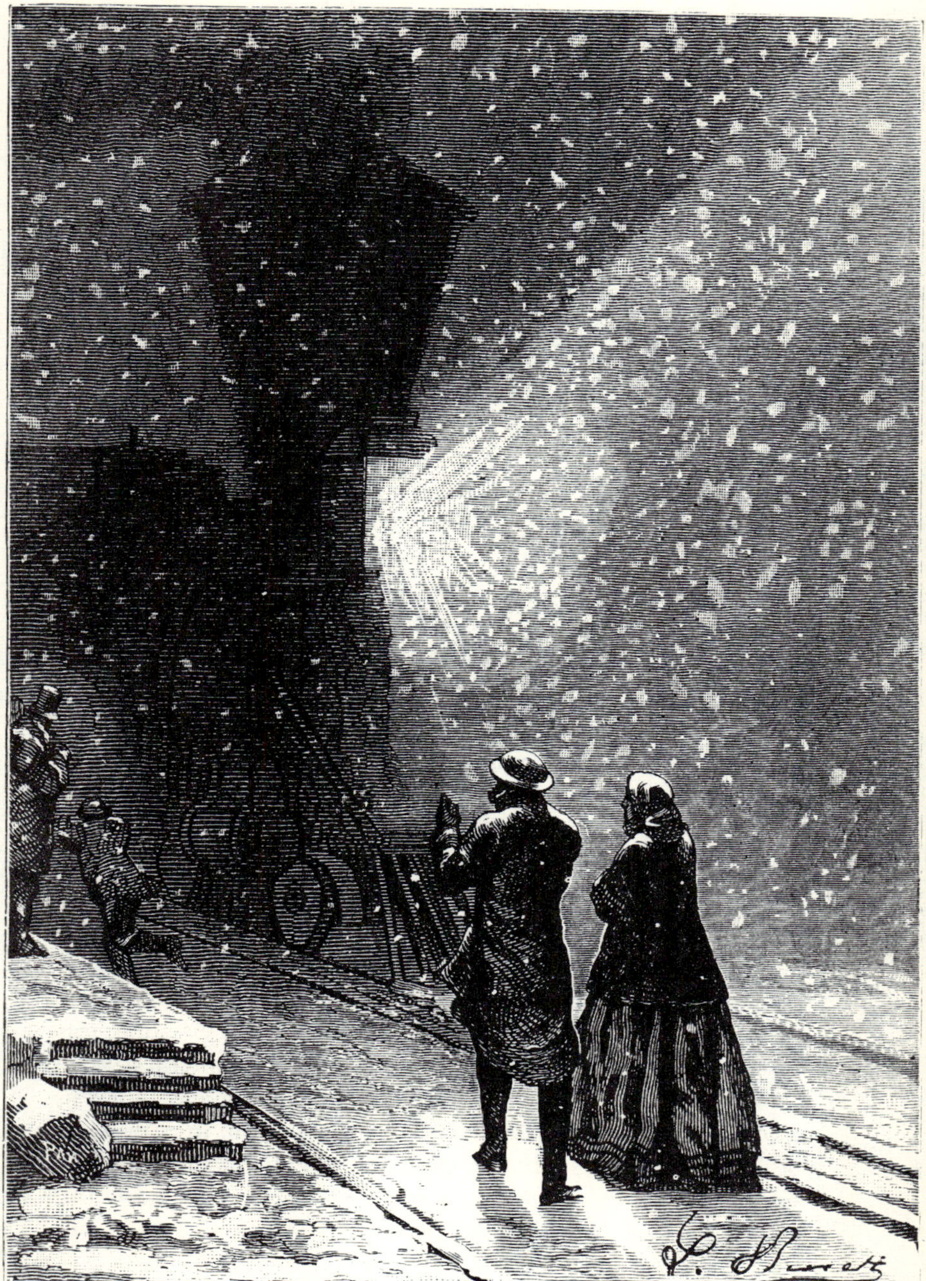

whereas the pictures of the end of the nineteenth century were really impregnated with the poetics of the text. One may verify this in another great collection of books for children of the period: the *Bibliothèque Rose*. In particular the illustrations of the works of the Comtesse de Ségur show to what degree the illustrator draws the very substance of the picture from the text. Not content with presenting the scene or the characters, he interprets the elements of the story with a militant passion. The sketch is no longer a picture of reality, but a moral and moralizing vision of things.

Certain engravings by Castelli offer excellent examples of this point. In *Jean qui grogne, Jean qui rit* Castelli picks out two sentences from the same speech, sentences which are not of themselves imagistic, but rather theological and abstract: "The devil who is evil and who makes you unhappy... God who keeps you and protects you day and night"; he then builds on the spirit of these two sentences several visual representations accessible to the child, taken from his daily psychological universe. Unhappiness, Hell, is for the child to be tied to the wall by a rope and to be unable to reach the sweets in front of him in spite of all his efforts: it is the torture of desire which cannot be satisfied. The horror of this engraving, comic but basically sadistic, appeals to the physical sensibility of the child. We know how essential the world of food is to the child, and consequently privation really constitutes a hell for him. The children attached to the wall are horribly ugly, which is normal in the logic of the manichean morality of Mme de Ségur and Castelli; they are bad and the Devil must necessarily make them unhappy.

We should note that the devil is represented only as a toy: a puppet devil springing from a box. This is certainly the sign of a religious tabu but it is not without some irony. This extraordinarily strong psychological picture, — strong because it calls forth a heard echo at the level of the child's interests and preoccupations — reveals a considerable perversity which is certainly not absent from the work of the Comtesse de Ségur. The illustration is thus faithful to the very spirit of the work; Castelli has not only understood the system used by the Countess, he has entered into it.

« Le diable qui est très méchant et qui vous rend malheureux. »

After the image of Hell, the child who reads *Jean qui grogne, Jean qui rit* deserves the compensatory image of supreme happiness. To illustrate the phrase "God who keeps you and protects you day and night" Castelli again lets himself go in interpretation. In place of an impossible picture of God he substitutes a guardian angel, a creation of the Saint-Sulpician catechism (one must not forget that Mme de Ségur was the friend of Veuillot, a journalist and *ultra* writer, and that it was at his insistence that she began to write). The angel enfolds a stylish cradle with her wings, where, under garlands of flowers, a child is sleeping. In her clothing, face and hair, the angel seems very feminine and she seems to be the idealized figure of the mother: the presence of the angel and of protective material warmth are one. The confusion of happiness, the sacred and security give an evident force to this image; it is constructed of the mythological and psychological elements in which the child of the Second Empire was saturated.

All the engravings and all the drawings of the *Magasin d'Éducation et de Récréation* and the *Bibliothèque Rose* were of course in black and white, since the picture album as such had not yet appeared in France. With the appearance of color, new forms of children's books developed at the same time as engraving became more rare and finally disappeared. The illustrated book lost much by this, but picture books for small children could henceforth utilize more varied techniques; a new era in the history of children's books began.

In 1933, Jean de Brunhoff published *The Story of Babar the Little Elephant,* the first link in a series of albums universally known. It must be said that the first of all these books is also the most perfect. The phenomenon of a series in the realm of children's books, as in all realms, exhausts, if not the theme, at least the graphic imagination of the author, and one arrives at mass production which runs the risk of leading to the stereotype deprived, at the least, of the spark of the beginning.

The large format of *Babar,* the use of colors and most of all the rigorous correspondence between the text and the picture (the text being conceived as support for an illustration much richer than the

Marion Durand

text itself) make an inseparable whole of *Babar,* and, in other words, the first *picture book* for children. The illustrations in *Babar* are never reducible to an arbitrary juxtaposition of diverse elements; they are always constructed and absolutely composed. The organization of space is really remarkable: the double page has been discovered and thus also the primordial importance of layout. In *Babar* the illustration is never compact; it breathes because it includes empty spaces which do not give the impression of holes but rather an area of possible movement. There is no vanishing perspective to narrow the field of vision (except when perspective indicates a departure); the landscapes are composed of successive, equalized planes which give the sensation of a world which is vast but without unknown elements, hence never frightening.

The picture is often constructed along a diagonal and it is relatively symmetrical. It was a challenge to frame within the page, and the child's vision, masses as gigantic as elephant-characters while cheating as little as possible with proportions, and in maintaining their harmony. The drawing of *Babar* is simple and linear, line is never gratuitous, it always delimits masses or zones of color. There is no fuzziness, the forms are demarcated and therefore perceived in their totality. Babar himself is a neutral gray but nevertheless it is he one sees first because he is always intelligently placed at that point of the picture where the eye of the reader first falls.

In the first book Jean de Brunhoff used only gray, red, green and yellow. Without blue, by playing with shades of red, pink and green, he was able to create a universe where one did not even notice the absence of that color. The success of *Babar,* which is the key book to which children return again and again, can be explained by the poetic and secure atmosphere of this universe more real than reality, a universe of rounded maternal forms, of soft colors, of a gentleness which is never too honeyed. We should note in passing that this soft padded material framework, still simple because it is devoid of gadgets, is a perfect projection of the ideal middle class life between 1930-1936 in France; tourism, a second house, and even the form of government, an elected monarchy. On the graphic as well as the emotional level, the pictures of collective life in the land of elephants are extremely comforting; each one recognizes his peers and lives with them without conflict.

This book, the first of the series, and in many ways a work of genius, is engraved in the memories and childhood sensibilities of many by virtue of the diversity and unity of its illustrations, the fitting tone, and that warmth which the whole work exudes. One can't remark without sadness the impoverishment and commercial exploitation of *Babar* at the present time, on television or in completely degraded albums done "in the manner" of Jean de Brunhoff.

At the same time that *Babar* appeared, an experiment in educational publishing, that of "Père Castor," began its long existence; the experiment continues today: some 400 albums have been published in forty years, all of them conceived by a single pedagogical idea, one new, rich and absolutely rigorous, the idea of Paul Faucher. This pedagogical adventure parallels the new education movement: the foundation of all Père Castor's work is the search for the concrete and for the tangible. The book should therefore encourage the infant to activity, serve as a bond between the child and nature, and the objects of daily life, while in fact it usually has acted as a screen between the child and reality. What was needed was to modify the behavior of the child confronted by the book, and to accomplish this the external aspect of the book as well as the contents had to be changed so that it might become an affective object which the child could handle as he pleased.

There are different collections (the *Story of the Beasts, Children of the Earth, Cigalou, First Readings, Second Readings*) which have been created and conceived by a tightly-knit team of psychologists, folklorists, ethnologists, naturalists, designers and illustrators. Before the war artists like Nathalie Parrain, Rojankovski, Helene Guertik, Angèle Malclés and Pierre Belvès contributed to opening horizons in the French picture book, to give it a certain dignity, to affirm its style.

In a lecture given at the inaugural meeting of the Fifth Congress of the International Union for Literature for Youth at Florence in

Marion Durand

1958, Paul Faucher said: "...by its original force, the illustration does not limit itself to informing the eyes and the intelligence; it touches also the sensibility and the imagination — child of motion, the illustration incites the human child to movement and action, child of observation, it incites the human child to observation and reflection, it stimulates thought."

Rojankovski, the artist for *Cigalou,* knew how to create characters, how to give them a certain presence and reality; Cigalou appears as a child of flesh and bone with tousled hair, who gets mud on his overshoes just like a real country child. The universe in which he develops is a universe where objects have thickness and color; these objects are always recognizable, the elements of the drawing are outlined with a clear line; forms are delimited and precise, never elliptical: the reader at once has an immediate and global vision, satisfying even independently of the text. In fact for Père Castor, "the illustration is autonomous, it has a meaning complete in itself, it carries a message."

Is it because the team of illustrators of the period before the war lost the best of its collaborators? Is it because team work became difficult? Because a necessary renovation was not accomplished in methods and style? Whatever the cause, during the past few years the albums of Père Castor seem to have been unable to free themselves from a heavy style lacking freedom and poetry. The illustrations are lustreless and compact, limited to the same horizon, without regard for the new space discovered by mechanics and by speed; they are always the same and yet inferior; they have become pedagogically inoffensive stereotypes which are plastically impoverished. Conceived according to principles which are still correct, these "albums" appear today to be unadapted to reality and to the child's vision of the world of 1969.

Except for a few rare sensitive and original books, nothing valuable has appeared during these last few years in France for children. The picture book market has been invaded and blocked by an enormous commercial production. A poverty of themes, pretention and idiocy of illustrations seem, for the moment, to condemn the French children's book to continue its current boring mediocrity.

In the nineteenth century engravers and sketchers such as Doré, Bennett, and Froelich were recognized by society, they existed by and could live off their work. If illustrators had a decent social and professional status in France today, perhaps the children's book would arouse a new form of creative imagination and take on new life.

Translated by Diana Wormuth.

André Winandy

The twilight zone: Imagination and reality in Jules Verne's *Strange Journeys*

With the moon's surface seen on every family television screen, the lag between idea and reality growing shorter, science seemingly catching up with the imagination, Verne's *Strange Journeys* fortunately are not yet historical fiction. They have not yet lost their appeal. Even if by-passed or proven wrong, his narratives convey as much as ever the fascination of the "worlds known and unknown," inspiring the young at heart with their longing for adventure in the real world as well as in the world of the imagination. Indeed the twilight zone is very much alive.

Known to some as a writer of compelling adventure stories, a "dreamer," a "seer," the "magician" of science fiction, Jules Verne has recently been reread and studied by literary critics. They have analyzed his sources and influences, exposed his writing to psychoanalytical investigation, and Marxist critics have even sorted out the anti-capitalistic, anti-imperialistic, anti-establishment elements in his fiction. [1]

---

[1] Among the most noteworthy criticism on Verne and his works are the following:
Andreev, Cyrille, "Préface des Œuvres complètes en U. R. S. S.," translated in *Europe,* April-May 1955.
L'Arc, no. 29, 1966, special volume on Jules Verne.
Butor, Michel, "Le point suprême et l'âge d'or à travers quelques œuvres de Jules Verne," *Arts et Lettres,* no. 15 (a special volume on Jules Verne), reprinted in *Répertoire,* Paris, 1960.
Evans, Idrisyn Oliver, *Jules Verne and his Work,* London, 1965.
Marcucci, Edmondo, *Guilio Verne e la sua opera,* Milan, 1930.
Moré, Marcel, *Le très curieux Jules Verne: le problème du père dans les "Voyages Extraordinaires,"* Paris, 1960.
———, *Nouvelles explorations de Jules Verne: musique, misogamie, machine,* Paris, 1963.
Popp, Max, *Julius Verne und sein Werk,* Hartleben, 1909.

Who is to say that he has discovered the real Jules Verne... the critic or the reader? In an effort to rediscover the "authentic" Jules Verne, let us reread Verne's texts with the enthusiasm of the young reader of Hetzel's *Magasin d'Éducation et de Récréation* where Verne's *Strange Journeys* were first published. To him Verne's narratives unfold vast and unexplored worlds of distant lands and open space. Attributing to the dynamism of their heroes the practical application of science, they project future discoveries and adventures in the four domains which men have always dreamed of conquering: the air, the earth, fire and water. They take him into the bowels of the earth and to the wonders of the deep sea, into "Worlds Known and Unknown," as Verne's collected *Strange Journeys* later were dramatically subtitled. For him, as for us today, Verne's fiction creates the realm of the twilight zone, a fusion of the imaginary and the real.

The Journey.

Jules Verne's plots are few and often borrowed, but they always present variations on the one basic thematic structure of the journey. Apart from the evident symbolic dimension of the *Strange Journeys*, there is a systematic geographical and planetary organization in Vernian travels with their itineraries charted in, around and on the surface of the globe. [2]

The journey itself reaches into the twilight zone where imagination and reality are fused. Travel is movement and contrasts with repose or rest. Travel is adventure, discovery, escape, liberation of the imagination, dream and poetry. One could well establish an entire psychology of travel in the Vernian narrative with its spiral or linear movement, projected in space and in time, and with its cyclic form. The setting of the extraordinary voyage is always exceptional

---

[2] Verne's master plan, as well as that of Hetzel's *Magasin d'Éducation et de Récréation,* was to sum up all the knowledge that had been amassed by modern science and to rework it in an imaginative and exciting history of the universe. "Avertissement de l'Éditeur," *Voyages extraordinaires, Voyages et aventures du capitaine Hattéras* (Paris, 1867), p. ii. This is Hetzel's first volume of the *Strange Journeys.*

and takes therefore itself the aspect of adventure: the great North, the deep sea, the volcano. ... As for time, the traveler and the reader leave the known for the unknown and return finally to the known and familiar world, reintegrating themselves with the familiar which they have only temporarily left behind. The cycle also represents an apprenticeship, for the traveler learns through his experiences and his exposure to new worlds. Through the journey the familiar themes of children's literature are expounded: departure and travel, the obstacles and trials which the hero overcomes, the triumph of the just and the punishment of the wicked, the conscious identification between reader and hero, etc....

In three of his adventures Verne takes to the skies as the ideal way to pass into the twilight zone. In *Hector Servadac,* when a meteorite hits the earth, a fragment breaks away and is thrown into the atmosphere and into orbit. The reader and the heroes accompany this satellite as it breaks out of the earth's atmosphere and crosses the solar system, while never leaving Gallia, this fragment of the earth in orbit. The mind's eye is opened to the cosmic world visible from the satellite and to new experiences and sensations of atmospheric conditions in outer space, but the perspectives of the imaginary are still bound to the familiar world of reality, for Gallia is after all a fragment of the earth. The field of the imagination narrows and the space travelers reintegrate more and more with reality as they return to earth where the cycle of the journey is completed.

In *From the Earth to the Moon* and *Round the Moon,* Verne remains closer to reality in his detailed and rigorous descriptions of the preparation for the launch as well as the subsequent carefully documented explanations for the landing's failure. Nevertheless he appeals very strongly to the reader's imagination and the attraction of the distant in the fantasies of the moon landscapes, the strange experiences of weightlessness, the spectacle of the earth seen from outer space and that of the disintegration of a meteorite close to the space capsule.

In a completely different realm, Professor Lidenbrock of *Journey to the Center of the Earth* travels largely to satisfy his scientific curiosity, but his young nephew Axel is motivated by excitement which is founded in both the real and the imaginary. There is a fascination in reality for Axel who enjoys the exhausative preparations and the detailed geological study at the core of the earth when he and his uncle analyze the strata. From the beginning of the adventure, however, Axel's imagination is captured by the almost mystical presence of a mysterious traveler who had preceded them to the center of the earth. A manuscript has identified the mysterious Saknussemm and the travelers literally follow in his footsteps in anticipation, incessantly feeling or sensing his presence. This "présence d'autrui," this spiritual presence of the other which accompagnies the journey and the characteristic thrill which it incites, is ever present in the symbols found along the travel route: the cryptogram at the entrance of the volcano where Lidenbrock and Axel begin their descent, the runic characters Arne Saknussemm carved in rock in the subterranean depths of the earth. In various Vernian novels similar symbols signal the mysterious presence of others who have preceded or who later will enter into the journey: the initials A. D. which the balloon travelers find on a rock in the heart of Africa (*Five Weeks in a Balloon*) as well as the many bottle messages fished from the sea in such novels as *Hector Servadac,* the *Mysterious Island* and the *Eternal Adam.*

The "mark of the Other" is not only an evocation of the past, it is a link between present, past and future. It moves the narrative and the reader imperceptibly into the nowhereland of timelessness. The resting place of the dead ships and the ruins of lost Atlantis in *Twenty Thousand Leagues under the Sea* transport the journey outside of time for a moment. It is almost as if the journey were at a standstill, as if past and future were incorporated in the very experience of the journey, in that of the traveler, and beyond the narrative, in that of the reader drawn up in its cycle. This is perhaps nowhere so strongly felt as when the impressionable reader descends with Axel and his companions into the innermost depths of the earth to witness not only the prehistoric rock formations, but its flora and

André Winandy

fauna, prehistoric man, the Protean guardian of a herd of mastadons and the duel of the preduluvian monsters. However the traveler does not dwell for long upon this twilight zone, for preoccupied with his journey, he moves on in time and in space. The privileged moment (outside of time) unfolds before his inner eye without his really participating in it, almost as if he were removed from the scene taking place in front of his eyes. He is watching as the reader is watching, removed or separated from the actual scene. Witness of the timelessness without being a part of it, the hero is thrown back into time as he continues his exploration, as is his reader as well. A further illustration can be taken from the *Eternal Adam,* which concludes Verne's posthumous collection *Yesterday and Tomorrow.* Its period is the indefinite future, its scene the site of a lost Atlantis. Here an aged philosopher deciphers a narrative from beyond the tomb, the history of a past civilization, buried ages before by one of its last survivors. Reader and decoder are thrown simultaneously into two dimensions of time. The reader of the novel obviously is facing forward, looking into the future. The decoder according to the narrative and its own reality faces backward reading into the past. The relative reality or unreality of time is further stretched by the multiple and revolving vantage points of the reader, who while reading a narrative, which takes place in the future, actually is also reading in the narrative, together with the decoder (story within a story, time within time), an historical document, an account of the passing of his own civilization. This disappearance of a second Atlantis, which lies in the past in relation to the decoder, is nevertheless future for the reader. As a result the reader, together with the old philosopher, is able to transcend time and imagine throughout the infinity of time the passing of all things in the universe and gain an intimate understanding of the time wheel, the eternal recurrence of events. There are for the reader three dimensions of reality. He is fascinated by his own reality (he is reading the novel), the fictional reality of the decoder (he is deciphering the message of a past civilization) and the reality of the message from this past civilization itself. The three dimensions converge for the reader who is no longer able to distinguish between fiction and fact. Verne has really succeeded in creating the twilight zone where the real and the imaginary fuse and come alive for the young, imaginative reader. The twilight zone exists in the fiction as well as in the mind or reaction of the reader himself.

Yet another aspect of the presence of the Other along the journey and its ramification in time is the narrative device of alluding to earlier novels and having their narratives act upon one another. In the *Mysterious Island* trilogy a double reference to previously published novels explains the mysterious help which the castaways have repeatedly received. A mutineers seaman whom Lord Glenarvan had marooned on a neighboring desert island in the *Children of Captain Grant* is responsible for many of the favors. His existence and identity revealed, he continues to help them fight off an attack of the pirates, his former mates. When the pirateer in turn is unexplainably blown up by a submarine, as the castaways and the readers learn in time, the underwater engine is commandeered by none other than Captain Nemo from *Twenty Thousand Leagues under the Sea*. Allusions such as these not only allow the author to tie up some of the loose ends of his narratives, but, most important, they give his story a new depth and perspective within its very world by bringing the strange and new in closer focus, by projecting it into the world of the familiar, of the known, in fiction and beyond the fiction in the actual world or reality of the reader.

By introducing in the unfolding narrative an already authenticated character from a previous story, with an identity, a life of his own, with whose past and stature the reader is familiar, the interior distance which separates the make-believe world of the heroes from the authentic world of the reader is dramatically narrowed. Furthermore the heroes of the narrative, the castaways themselves, are readers who know the new hero because they have read the previous Vernian adventures, a circumstance which further blurs the distinction between fiction and reality. Reader and hero share the common experience of a new reality, namely that of the narrative, wherein the reappearing familiar hero, the fictional hero-reader (who has read their story and becomes involved with them in his own adventure) and the actual reader (who, though outside of the narratives, identifies with both the fictional hero-

André Winandy

reader and the reappearing familiar hero) are so closely fused in the twilight zone that the imaginary and the real form only one common dimension.

Another "présence d'autrui" in the Vernian journey, although of a different nature, and equally accepted in both the world of the real and the imaginary, is the presence of Providence. At times acting as a silent partner on the journey by its mere presence, the notion of the Divine is a reassuring, comforting agent for the traveler. The latter expresses his faith in moments of crisis, commending himself to divine Providence or giving thanks to God where appropriate. Occasionally Providence intervenes directly in the adventure. During a storm the passengers of the "Dobryna" (*Hector Servadac*) fear that their ship will be thrown against a wall of rocky cliffs. Their only hope rests in divine intervention. The ship and passengers are in fact saved miraculously as a passageway opens before them just in time, for the clever seamanship of the Russian captain would have been insufficient otherwise. Verne's sincere religious faith in divine Providence, while transcending his basic scientific determinism, is nevertheless easily accepted as transmitted truth by the youthful reader, free from metaphysical concerns. Although divine Providence enters the world of the journey, the traveler is in general silent about his personal religious beliefs. This was in accord with Hetzel's desire to keep his *Magasin d'Education et de Récréation* free from all sectarian bias, while still giving it a sound moral and religious basis.

Among the "présences d'autrui" in Verne's novels, the presence of women in the journey is mostly external and irrelevant or at times completely lacking. Women enter very little into the journey, because romance is outside both the hero's and the young reader's world of adventure. Generally the woman is present at static moments at the start and at the term of the journey. She represents the home, the family, and thus only the real world. What is more important, no journey is ever undertaken in quest of a woman. Even in the *Carpathian Castle*, the presence of the woman, far from having any rapport with Novalis, the "Romantik" or the "eternal feminine," is but an accessory to the main mystification and could be replaced by other catalysts. After all "la Stilla" is dead, and her seemingly supernatural presence as well as that of the mysterious voices are explained by the use of concave mirrors and voice recordings.

While still caught up in the mirage of the mark of the Other, the interest of the hero-travelers in *Twenty Thousand Leagues Under the Sea* shifts at times from the strange exploration to the strange explorer himself, in whose journey they have become involved. The very ambiguity of Captain Nemo, his identity and his mysterious past, place him between two worlds: the reality of the fiction and the imagination of the hero-travelers with whom the reader identifies. Far from being a simple mechanical blueprint without any psychological depth, Nemo, like many of Verne's characters, represents a deliberate attempt by the author to create a "Gestalt" for the imagination of his younger reader. The meaningful symbol is never completely separate from the make-believe world. The very flatness of the character with whom the reader empathizes serves a formative, didactic purpose: his sympathy with revolt against tyranny, his thirst for self-justification and the final crying out of his conscience to God. He, his voyage, his descent into the sea and the sea itself become symbolic, the very personification of freedom.

This didacticism which keeps the symbol suspended between the real and the imaginary also applies to the occasional portrayal of the scientist as a villain, in order to illustrate the dangers of "science without conscience." Sane at his worst such as Herr Schultze and Robur who disregard human lives, insane like Thomas Roch, or an unbalanced lunatic like Marcel Camaret who is used by others, the scientist is often physically defective. The members of the Gun Club have cracked skulls and artificial limbs and Ofranik lacks eyes. The scientist is in any event always somewhat outside of the adventure and never the principal hero of the journey with whom the reader identifies. Nor does he ever reach the term of the journey. The enigmatic Robur, having become the personification of evil in *Master of the World,* deliberately flies into the heart of an electrical storm in blasphemous challenge to all forces including the supernatural. His ship, "L'Épouvante," is struck by lightening and Robur is smitten by divine will. In a similar way Herr Schultze succumbs to his demonic devices, while Thomas Roach destroys himself. The villain out of the story, the way is paved for the authentic hero to leave the realms of the marvelous, intersection of myth and reality, and to complete his journey.

The twilight zone of reader, hero, and fiction is certainly not created to intimidate but rather to impart through the imaginary a positive lesson for the real world of hero and reader, rejecting any unjustified fear of the unexplainable. Far from being obsessed by the search for a privileged place to withdraw to (the North pole, a desert island, the heart of a volcano) where he would be free from the anguish of evil, [3] the authentic hero and the reader find freedom in the story itself. If Jules Verne's adventurer explores the known and the unknown of his planet, it is in order to dominate it and to make it serve him better. From the twilight zone the traveler always comes back into the dimension of fictional reality which parallels that of the imaginative reader. Thus imagination serves the real. Verne, perpetually fascinated with the underlying explanation of all phenomena, transforms the imaginary into the plausible and blends basic plot, imagination and reality in the charismatic formula of his *Journeys*. No factor ever remains to puzzle the imagination or to destroy thus the illusion of the fictional reality. This illusion is always kept alive and the explanation becomes dynamic didacticism within the realms of the imaginary, the fictive and the real. The thematic device of the journey into "worlds known and unknown" permits him to pass incessantly between two domains, from that of the known and the real, to that of the imagined and the imaginary. He effects this passage from the imaginary to the positivist description while always maintaining verisimilitude by creating the impression that the extraordinary is possible and indeed probable: the imaginary is always explained, the hypothesis is always proven scientifically possible, the journey can always be charted.

---

[3] Michel Butor, "Le point ...," *Répertoire*, pp. 130-162.

The twilight zone

Graphic Language.

Many a Vernian reader can recall, even though he was less sensitive to the author's language as an adolescent, the fascination of the illustrated cryptogram. Here the image, a representation of reality, becomes reality itself. No doubt equally vivid to him is the memory of his leafing through a novel of Verne, pouring over the illustrations, turning the pages, his curiosity now aroused, and reading this story within a story as told to him page by page through the illustrations alone. Faithfully reflecting the story and its lessons, the illustrations portray the characters, situate the action and depict the important moments of the journey. In addition, the image adds to the story, for this journey by picture combines the effect of legend and illustration, be it by simple identification of the characters and scenes portrayed or by descriptive or narrative quotations from the text itself. The total context blends to inspire the reader's "imagination," "dreams," or "evasion."

Realistic, but drawn from an imagined reality differing from that of the known and unknown worlds of the globe, the meaning and mystery of the illustration do not stem from the mere representation of an event already well described in the text, but from the inclusion of everything that surrounds it. Describing or delineating the voyage, the illustration thus becomes the journey itself.

The same is true of Verne's image, the description within the text. His description is the total staging of a dramatic representation. He dramatizes landscape by transforming it into a magic lantern of color and shapes which unfold before the traveler's and the reader-spectator's enthralled eyes. Even after a rapid reading, the underwater fields that the reader has crossed in Captain Nemo's "Nautilus" and the regions of the Great North and the Antarctic he has seen on his way to the north pole with Captain Hatteras seem as familiar to him as to the explorers who have in fact made this voyage.

The fictional image becomes reality through Verne's skillful use of graphic language. The sense of immediacy which emanates from

Une fenêtre ouverte sur ses abîmes inexplorés (p. 103).

The twilight zone

Verne's descriptions of the sea, the desert, the jungle and the icefields, the depth of his three-dimensional vision which he underscores with various lighting effects convey to the fellow traveler, which the reader has become, a kaleidoscopic impression of the known and unknown worlds where representation and invention fuse, where object and reflection of object combine to form a well-composed life-like tableau:

> The rays of the sun struck the surface of the waves at rather an oblique angle, and at the touch of their light, decomposed by refraction as through a prism, flowers rocks, plants, shells, and polypi were shaded at the edges of the seven solar colours. It was marvelous, a feast for the eyes, this complication of coloured tints, a perfect kaleidoscope of green, yellow, orange, violet, indigo, and blue; in one word, the whole palette of an enthusiastic colourist! [4]

Jules Verne expands his multifaceted projection, taking the reader into the wonders of make-believe, helping him to forget that he is imparting information:

> Various kinds of isis, clusters of pure tuft-coral, prickly fungi, and anemones, formed a brilliant garden of flowers, enamelled with porphitae, decked with their collarettes of blue tentacles, sea-stars studding the sandy bottom, together with asterophytons like fine lace embroidered by the hands of naïads, whose festoons were waved by the gentle undulations caused by our walk. [5]

The fascination and spell of these descriptions are the result of successive, superimposed impressions which combine exact observation and scientific documentation with a powerful imagination which nevertheless is guided by a rational element controlling it. Beyond the documentary, Verne succeeds in rendering experience beautiful, familiar though distant.

---

[4] *Twenty Thousand Leagues under the Sea* (New York, 1952), p. 102.
[5] *Ibid.*, pp. 102-103.

André Winandy

With all of the richness of the externals, Jules Verne's description is somewhat disappointing nevertheless because of the overpowering excess of the objective element. His fiction is a fiction of the object. His worlds, known and unknown, often seem to reduce themselves to shimmering matter in motion. By narrowing the field of vision of the make-believe, however, and thus opening the inner eye of the reader to it, Verne succeeds in narrowing the distance between object and consciousness of the object. He always places an unknown in conjunction with a known impression, juxtaposing a new sight to a common, familiar, everyday correspondence. He compares Mount Rawlinson's cascades, cataracts and avalanches to the thunder of heavy artillery fire (*The Adventures of Capitain Hatteras*). To evoke the peace and emptiness of the same scene under moonlight, he compares the rock and ice formation to tombstones and imparts the impression of an immense treeless cemetery where twenty generations of the whole world are sleeping an eternal slumber. In order to immerse the reader in the magic of the underwater landscape in *Twenty Thousand Leagues under the Sea,* Verne constantly compares the fictional reality to authentic experiences of the reader:

> Fishes got up under our feet like birds in the long grass... Millions of luminous spots shone brightly in the midst of the darkness. They were the eyes of giant crustacea crouched in their holes; giant lobsters setting themselves up like halberdiers, and moving their claws with the clicking sound of pincers; titanic crabs, pointed like a gun on its carriage; and frightful looking poulps, interweaving their tentacles like a living nest of serpents. [6]

Various phenomena become thus direct and immediate experience.. The description becomes a kind of living theater where participation of the reader is forced.

Conscious of reader and fiction, Verne uses an array of narrative devices to capture and hold his imagination at the intersection of myth

---

[6] *Ibid.,* p. 248.

and reality. In his use of the "narrator," to study only one of his many techniques, Verne, not unlike Balzac, uses in addition to the obvious dramatized narrators (the heroes of the journey) the usual disguised narrators: the implied undramatized narrator and a host of narrator agents. Among these are outside observers, who intervene temporarily in the narrative and then fade away giving the impression of dimensional depth. The implied narrator confers at the same time the impression of an unmediated story, in which the reader is absorbed. This illusion of an unidentifying vision, this magic realm of the fictional world and the real world is further enlarged by the various centers of consciousness through whom the author has filtered his narrative. They serve as mirrors reflecting the mental experiences of the reader, or camera eyes of the imaginary zooming in on the reader's capacity for visualization.

On the other hand Verne draws the reader even closer within the narrative by breaking through the fictional boundaries, making him witness the unfolding of the adventure. Inserts of blocks of information and of "authentic" documents like a concert program sheet, a menu, newspaper clippings, timetables, inventories, bearings and mathematical equations, also create the impression of immediacy, of unmediated participation in the fiction. Thus the twilight zone is kept alive somewhere, between a vision of long ago and the reality of today.

Translated by Rita Winandy.

Jean Chesneaux

Jules Verne's image of the United States

Jules Verne's aim in writing his adventure stories was not just to entertain his young readers but to make them think about the world around them. His novels were first published in serial form in the suggestively titled *Magasin d'Éducation et de Récréation,* edited by Hetzel (Verne's spiritual father, according to Marcel Moré [1]) with Verne himself as co-director. Verne's works are entitled *Les Voyages extraordinaires* and subtitled *Les Mondes connus et inconnus,* which in itself indicates that he wanted not only to stimulate the imagination of his young audience but also to interest them in one of his own favorite preoccupations: the connection between the past and the future, between the real and the possible. He combed the society of his time for clues pointing to the future development of humanity. Man, he believed, would become progressively more and more capable of mastering nature, of extending his dominion over the earth. There is, therefore, an underlying unity between his science fiction on the one hand, and his political and social novels on the other.

This is why the American character and society of the nineteenth century fascinated him. He saw America as the frontier linking the "known and unknown worlds." The United States was very much a part of the contemporary political scene and the Civil War, in particular, had made a deep impression on this young middle-class liberal, born in 1828. But at the same time, this country, in the throes of rapid demographic, technical, and economic change, with few real ties to the past, had already become a major futuristic

---

[1] See Marcel Moré, *Le très curieux Jules Verne* (Paris, 1964).

theme. In the mid-nineteenth century, it was the United States which came the closest to the "model for progress" that Jules Verne envisioned for humanity. As such, it provided an ideal setting for his scientific and social prefigurations. America falls neatly into Jules Verne's projection, and it is hardly by coincidence that twenty-three out of a total of sixty-four novels take place in part or entirely on American soil, and that important roles are given to American characters.

In this country where everything seemed possible, the child's imagination was at ease. Children could give free rein to their sense of adventure and to their natural enthusiasm for progress, freedom, and work. For the generations of young Frenchmen whom Verne was addressing, America would always be the home of Fenimore Cooper and his pioneers. Verne himself, like all the young people of his time, had been brought up on Cooper: his father used to read the *Leather Stocking Tales* every evening to the family circle. But the United States was also the country of technical progress which children dreamt of. There the young are given the responsibilities of grown men. Such is the case of young Harbert, one of the five heroes of *The Mysterious Island*. Already at the age of fifteen his knowledge as a naturalist is indispensable for the survival of the "Castaways of the Air."

The United States is the land of born mechanics and engineers for Verne. "The Yankees are the first and foremost technicians of the world; they are engineers in the same way as the Italians are musicians and the Germans metaphysicians, by birth." What could be more natural, after all, than that the project of sending a capsule to the moon should originate in the United States among the members of the Baltimore Gun Club? America is the land where modern industrial techniques flourish; it provides a favorable climate for the launching of the boldest projects. For the trip to the moon, all that is necessary is to calculate correctly the size of the cannon, and above all, to cast it. It is in Florida, for astronomical reasons, that the operation takes place. Jules Verne describes it in a chapter ("The

Fête of the Casting") which is a veritable lyric hymn to the glory of American metallurgy and to the Promethean powers of man:

> Twelve noon struck. The cannon shot burst suddenly and launched through the sky its fulvous flash. Twelve hundred melting troughs opened at once, and twelve hundred snakes of fire slithered toward the central well, unrolling all the while their incandescent coils. Once there, they plunged down a depth of nine hundred feet with a terrific roar. It was a moving and a magnificent sight! The earth trembled while these molten waves, ejecting toward the sky huge whirlwinds of smoke, volatized the moisture of the mould, and hurled it through the stone-lined vents in the form of impenetrable gases. These man-made clouds unrolled their thick spirals, climbing to a height of a thousand yards. Some savage wandering beyond the horizon would have been tempted to believe that a new crater was forming in the heart of Florida, but there was no eruption, no storm, no struggle of the elements — none of the terrible phenomena that nature is capable of producing. No! It was man, by himself, who had created those reddish fumes, those gigantic flames — worthy indeed of a volcano — those resounding vibrations similar to a severe earthquake, those reverberations which rival tempests and hurricanes. And it was his hand that precipitated into an abyss, dug out by him, a whole Niagara of molten metal. [2]

American society is seen by Verne as one in which scientific and technical problems are of concern to the man on the street corner. They belong to the people, rather than being set apart as they are in the Old World, in the dusty studies of the Academies and scholarly societies. The session at which the Weldon Institute of Philadelphia discusses the relative advantages of "heavier than air" and "lighter

---

[2] *De la terre à la lune*, pp. 91-92. (All quotations from Jules Verne's works are taken from the Hetzel edition of *Les Voyages extraordinaires*.)

than air" is as lively and as agitated as a political meeting; the engineer Robur, that prototype of the future American, has just demonstrated the superiority of his flying machines over balloons *(The Clipper of the Clouds)*. Robur's futuristic machines are American creations: *l'Albatros,* a kind of helicopter with multiple propellers fixed on vertical axes, and *l'Epouvante,* which moves with equal ease on land and in the air and water. Again, it is in the United States that Jules Verne places a number of his other scientific projections: for example, the *Propeller Island,* which takes American millionaires across the Pacific; or that delightful, whimsical Boston to Liverpool Pneumatic Tubes Co. which sends its passengers through the depths of the Atlantic at 1,800 kilometers an hour like an ordinary express letter. [3]

The United States for Verne is also the land *par excellence* of the railroad, that living imprint of man on the face of the earth, that signature by which he sets the mark of his superiority throughout entire continents. On the occasion of the inaugural trip of the "Great Trans-Asiatic Bakou-Peking," it is an American who in a burst of enthusiasm describes the railroads as "steel ribbons which will eventually encircle our earth as though it were no more than a hogshead or a bale of cotton." [4] The vast stretches of land in America provide a particularly favorable setting for the establishment of an immense iron network, which Phileas Fogg, for example, will use in order to win his bet in *Around the World in Eighty Days.* Going by the Pacific Railroad and the Mid-West lines, it takes him seven days to get from San Francisco to New York, by way of Omaha and Chicago. It is only because of an attack by the Sioux that he is delayed and misses his steamboat at New York.

The confrontation between man and nature that takes place in the United States is on a vaster scale than in Europe; it is also a more trying experience. Jules Verne had taken the traditional tour of the United States in 1867, complete with the standard boat trip

---

[3] This tale, *An Express of the Future,* is known only in the English version published in the *Strand Magazine* (July-December, 1895).
[4] *Claudius Bombarnac,* p. 19.

at dawn up the Hudson and a visit to Niagara Falls. (In those days, there was no talk of filling in the Hudson in order to construct an airport). This trip, which he transcribes almost literally in *A Floating City* (based on the gigantic steamship Great Eastern, which had taken him from Le Havre to New York), had made him physically aware of the vast scale of nature in America. Niagara Falls remained for him a symbol of the powerful forces of nature which confronted the young American republic. (He calls the casting operation referred to earlier, "a Niagara of molten metal"). In the novels of Verne's American cycle, *The Begum's Fortune, From the Earth to the Moon, Around the World in Eighty Days, North against South, The Will of an Eccentric,* and *Master of the World,* he dwells at length on the immense spaces of America, on the rich growth of its vegetation, on its geological resources — in short, on all that makes up the stakes in the struggle of man against nature.

The vision of the United States as a land of technical and economic progress fits directly into the tradition of French utopian socialism which flourished at the beginning of the nineteenth century, although Jules Verne is writing as much as a half century later (his earliest novel appeared in 1862). Basically, the Vernian project is very Saint-Simonian; for what could be a better résumé of the *Voyages extraordinaires* than the old Saint-Simonian injunction: "to go from the exploitation of man by man to the exploitation of nature by mankind." [5] *The Mysterious Island* is almost a kind of Saint-Simonian parable in its exaltation of work and science as the universal panacea. The "castaways of the sky" — who are, significantly, five Americans of the North fleeing from Richmond by balloon during the Civil War — manage to live off the island, thanks to their diligent efforts and the encyclopedic knowledge of their leader, Cyrus Smith.

It is well-known that the Saint-Simonians were very much interested in the United States, a country in which they discerned the propotype of a new society, freed from the political stagnation of

---

[5] See my article, "Jules Verne et la tradition du socialisme utopique." *L'Homme et la société,* No. 4, July 1967.

Europe and founded on technology. As René Rémond, who traces the history of the image of America in nineteenth century France, puts it, "With the United States begins a new chapter in human history: man ceases his submissive role, he begins to act on his environment, he learns to dominate the forces of nature, he exploits natural resources and transforms the world. He abandons resigned submission for active creativity." [6] Michel Chevallier, one of the most brilliant Saint Simonians, who was himself an engineer, had done first-hand research on the American railroads in 1836 and published a number of highly favorable works about American society. This Utopian socialist, who was to become an active businessman and a theorist of economic liberalism during the Second Empire, "was admirably equipped for understanding a society without a past, where the idle had no place, a society completely oriented toward work, efficiency, and the accumulation of capital, and where politics meant economics." [7] What Michel Chevallier admires about the United States, again according to René Rémond, "is basically its Saint-Simonian aspect: the freedom of industry, general productivity, the development of communications, the availability of credit — in short, all that would today be called economic expansion." [8]

Another aspect of Verne's image of America which belongs to utopian socialism is the experimental nature of the society he envisioned. It is well-known that all through the nineteenth century, the forward-looking men of the Old World dreamt of experimental microcosms of the perfect commonwealth, which, if successful, would then orient the whole of humanity along the road of progress. This was true in the case of Cabet, the French communist who published *Voyage en Icarie* in 1848. It was equally true of the Japanese Christian socialist, Sen Katayama, future director of the Komintern, who in 1905 had tried to create a model colony of Japanese peasants in the middle of Texas. Jules Verne is very much a part of the tradition of the "Imaginary Continent," as René Rémond aptly calls it. After

---

[6] René Rémond, *Les Etats-Unis devant l'opinion française (1815-1852)*. (Paris, 1962) 2 vols., p. 769.
[7] *Ibid.* p. 376.
[8] *Ibid.* p. 775.

the catastrophe which destroys the colony they were hoping to "offer to the Union government," the colonists of *The Mysterious Island* are able to found a model community, thanks to the gold left to them by Captain Nemo. The same thing happens in Oregon where two rival inheritors of the fabulous estate of the Begum found the rival cities of Franceville and Stahlstadt, both destined to explore paths for nature human development, but one in the direction of peace, the other in that of war. The choice of a setting is hardly accidental. Franceville, notes Verne, benefited from its location "within a federal republic and in a state still young, which allowed it to maintain a provisional independence with the proviso that it would become a part of the Union after a certain number of years." [9]

All these positive aspects of American society — the great industrial works, the mastery of nature, the sense of personal initiative and enterprise, the economic activity — are inseparable from a kind of Yankee national character (because for Verne, as we shall suggest, the United States means above all the Northern States, recently victorious in the Civil War). This particularly Yankee temperament is fashioned by an atmosphere of progress and success which was prevalent throughout the nation: "Nothing could take an American by surprise... in America, everything is delightfully simple, refreshingly easy, and as for mechanical difficulties, why, they are solved before they even arise." [10] The Yankee is a man of action, a man who succeeds: "A Yankee generally does not take the long way around; he takes the quickest road and usually the one which arrives at its goal." [11] The stupid rivalry and vanity which exist so often among people in the Old World are unheard of in the States. "When an American gets an idea, he finds another American who thinks as he does. If they are three, a president is elected and the other two are secretaries. With four, an archivist is appointed and the project is launched. With five, they call a general meeting and the club is formally constituted." [12]

[9] *Les 500 millions de la Begum*, p. 97.
[10] *De la terre à la lune*, p. 15.
[11] *Robur le conquérant*, p. 7.
[12] *De la terre à la lune*, p. 2.

Jules Verne's image of the United States

This Yankee character is not defined by psychological traits alone, but also by physical ones according to Verne. The new social and political conditions reached in the course of North American expansion in the nineteenth century had produced a new race of men, in the biological sense of the term. Verne was to return time and again to this idea in his *Voyages extraordinaires*. For example, he describes Cyrus Smith, the first-rate engineer from Massachusetts whose ingenuity saves the shipwrecked members of the *Mysterious Island* from death by starvation, as

> A real North American, thin, bony, lanky, around forty-five years old... He had one of those "numismatic" profiles which seem to have been made to be struck on a medal... With his ingenuity went a high degree of physical skill. He possessed fully the three qualities which together make up human energy: mental and physical activity, bold plans, will power. [13]

But the United States in the eyes of Jules Verne is not just the country of economic expansion and progress. It is also the land of liberty. This vision makes him at one with the French Americanophiles of the mid-nineteenth century, like De Toqueville and Michel Chevallier. To his way of thinking, it is this liberty "which is the basis of power for the Republic of the United States." [14] It is toward America that progressive men look, the enemies of conservative and authoritarian regimes. In the novel *A Family without a Name,* that perspicacious prefiguration of "Québec libre" (written in 1889), the French Canadian insurgents revolting against the British viceroy in Ottawa think of the United States across the Saint Lawrence as a promised land from which they can expect support. The novel takes place at the time of the anti-British agitation in Québec in 1837. Among the leaders of the French Canadian nationalists are Americans who give their allegiance to the spirit of Jefferson and to the Monroe Doctrine, and who wish to drive England from its last strongholds in the New World.

---

[13] *L'Ile mystérieuse*, p. 10.
[14] *Les 500 millions de la Begum*, p. 44.

Jean Chesneaux

The claims of the French Canadian revolutionaries are supported in the United States; they get their arms from Vermont. Their flag is white, in homage to their old homeland, but it bears in silhouette the American and Canadian eagles.

It is the Civil War, even more than the 1837 insurrection in Québec, which stimulates Jules Verne's sympathies for the United States as the land of liberty. This was "the war which brought about the triumph of justice and right." [15] He takes the side of "the North, the abolitionists, the unionists," against "the South, the slave owners, the secessionists, the confederates." [16] The four castaways of *The Mysterious Island* are abolitionists, and one of them, Smith's servant, is a black, who is treated as an equal by his four companions. Another American hero in Jules Verne's works is the good-natured painter, Max Réal, who is one of the participants in the "game of goose" stipulated by the strange testament of Hipperbone in *The Will of an Eccentric*. He almost worships John Brown, the pioneer of emancipation. [17] And among the heroes of liberty whose portraits hang in the study of Captain Nemo — the political heroes of Verne himself — we find the Italian Manin, the Greek Botzaris, the Pole Kosciusko, the Irishman O'Connell as well as three Americans (the number is proportionately significant): Washington, Lincoln and John Brown. The last is depicted "hanging from the gibbet, as Victor Hugo so terrifyingly sketched him." [18]

The Civil War also provided Jules Verne with the historical setting for an entire novel, *North against South,* a book in which a philanthropic plantation owner of Florida, James Burbank, frees his slaves right in the middle of the war, at the risk of provoking the

---

[15] *L'Ile mystérieuse,* p. 612.
[16] *Nord contre Sud,* p. 8.
[17] "John Brown, who flew the first flag of the abolitionists at the very beginning of the Civil War ... The Virginian plantation owners hunted him as if he were a wild animal. He had only a handful of men to support him ... after prodigious acts of courage, he was seriously wounded, reduced to helplessness, captured and dragged to neighboring Charleston, where he was hanged on December 2, 1859. It was a death over which the ignominy of the gibbet had no power; his fame and glory will remain from age to age. It is to this martyr of liberty, to this martyr of human freedom, that I wanted to pay homage as a patriot." *Le Testament d'un excentrique,* p. 346.
[18] *Vingt mille lieues sous les mers,* p. 283.

most horrible reprisals. His son, fighting in the ranks of the North, manages to call upon himself the hatred of the secessionist leader at Jacksonville, the Spanish-Seminole half-breed, Texar. All of the episodes in the novel serve as a pretext for Jules Verne to launch long arguments against slavery and appeals on behalf of the North. For him, slavery is the main issue at stake in the Civil War, much more than economic rivalry between North and South or the tariff question. With the typically idealistic position of the 1848 European liberal, Jules Verne saw the Civil War as having decided once and for all the Negro problem in the United States, insofar as it gave full legal rights to the former slaves.

The United States as the land of liberty is also the one in which the repressive machinery of the State and social constraints are the least felt. "The people of America know how to protect themselves without looking to the government for aid, which it is incapable of giving," declares Jules Verne with obvious satisfaction. [19] Elsewhere, with reference to the crowds of people at Baltimore who surround the future astronauts without excessive adulation, he speaks of "that liberty which characterizes those who are nurtured on the ideas of self-rule." [20] One of his novels in particular, *César Cascabel*, furnishes him with the pretext for illustrating the liberalism of the American state machinery, which he contrasts with the bureaucratic interferences and red tape of the czarist administration. The novel takes place in 1867, right at the time of the Alaskan Purchase. The Cascabel family, a band of itinerants, are trying to return to Europe from California by way of the Bering Straits. On their first try they had been driven back from Alaska by the Russian police because they lacked passports. On their second try, they found themselves in the presence of American authorities. "The Alaskan Purchase had been negotiated and signed just in time... on this land which had newly become American, there were no more of those stiff-necked bureau-

---

[19] *Le Testament d'un excentrique*, p. 3.
[20] *De la terre à la lune*, p. 9.

crats, no more of that red tape which so concerned the Moscovite administration." [21]

On the point of marriage and divorce, in particular, Jules Verne expressed special admiration for what René Rémond so aptly terms "the unimposing government." As Marcel Moré points out, Verne, a bit of a misogynist at heart, frequently allowed himself to make fun of the yoke of married life in his novels. [22] Marriage and divorce in the United States of his time appeared to him to be mere formalities which one could do away with at a moment's notice — an idea which received his full approval.

Thus, the flattering image that Verne formulated of the United States corresponds to his own political sympathies. America, in the midst of wide-scale economic expansion, spanned by a network of railroads (as the earth would one day be) has all the sympathy of this heir of the Saint-Simonian utopian socialism. A son of 1848, Verne found America appealing; for him, it was the land of liberty whose sole grave political crisis had been resolved, he thought, by the emancipation. And the discretion of the American political machine toward those under its jurisdiction had a secret charm for a man of his liberal and even anarchical sympathies. [23]

But gradually, as the development of industry aggravates human misery rather than relieving it, as the humanitarian dreams of 1848 are supplanted by the implacable rivalry of the various forms of imperialism, the highly idealistic view of Jules Verne gives way to pessimism. Forced to renounce the Saint-Simoniam vision of progress through science, Verne becomes a bitter, disappointed man. He sinks into a gloomy pessimism which colors the image he had formed of the United States. As the expansionist orientation of the Big Stick policy comes into play (Verne died in 1905), as the reign of the dollar establishes itself, as technology replaces humanism, he is forced to

---

[21] *César Cascabel,* p. 123.
[22] *Le très curieux Jules Verne,* p. 196.
[23] See my article, "Critique sociale et thèmes anarchistes chez Jules Verne." *Le Mouvement Social,* July 1966.

abandon his Jeffersonian and Lincolnian optimism and his admiration for a young, dynamic society.

In the beginning, the theme of the dollar is only discretely alluded to, for example, in *The Tribulations of a Chinese Gentleman* (1879). The hero, rich Kin-Fo, buys life insurance from a Chicago agency with a branch office in Shanghai, called "The Centenary." Two of the company's agents are to accompany him constantly, because a considerable sum of money is involved. But they abandon him at midnight in the middle of a desert, the contract having expired since the premiums are unpaid. In *The School for Crusoes* (1882), the criticism of the almighty dollar is still relatively discreet and humorous. Two millionaires from San Francisco, Kilderup and Taskinar, are fighting over a desert island, which the American government has put up for auction. A mock-heroic battle ensues "between the two strong-boxes" with dollars, instead of fists, flying. But the satire is still indulgent here.

By the time we get to *Propeller Island* (1895), the criticism of an American society based on money has become much more biting. This artificial island, which has all the mechanical devices necessary for comfort and efficiency (complete air conditioning, moving sidewalks, silent electric cars) sails throughout the Pacific. Built by a private American company, it admits only the richest millionaires as residents. The dollar during this period (the novel is supposed to take place in an undefined but relatively near future) is all-powerful and permits one to buy anything, even art and talent. "The Yankee invaders used gold to supply public and private galleries with European masters, both ancient and modern; they bought poets, musicians, and dramatists of talent. It was thus that they finally infused in themselves the feeling for beautiful and noble things — which they had lacked for so long." [24] Significantly, the authorities of the island have no scruples about kidnapping four French musicians, the "concert quartet," in order to assure its monopoly on art, with fabulous salaries amounting to a million gold francs per person per year.

---

[24] *L'Ile à Hélice*, p. 5.

Jean Chesneaux

At the head of the wealthy island society are two extremely rich rival families, the Coverleys and the Tankerdons, who are competing for control of the government of "Billionaire-City," the capital of the island. Tankerdon, a heavy-set merchant from the Middle West, is a coarse *nouveau riche,* while his rival, Coverley, seems to have retained a slight aura of refinement characteristic of the great Southern families in the early days. Here, for the first time, Jules Verne strays from his attitude of political solidarity with the North, expressed in the novel *North against South.* His anxiety in the face of increasing emphasis on purely material progress in the United States outweighs for once his liberal sympathies with the abolitionist North. Moreover, the cultural level of the island does not measure up to its financial power. "Even if teachers are paid the salaries of politicians, students hardly flock to the public courses, and if it is true that in the present generation the impact of studies in New England's colleges can still be felt, the generation that follows will certainly have less education than revenue." [25]

As might be expected, the leisure time of the island nabobs is not exactly devoted to intellectual pursuits: the librarian, with a stipend of $25,000.00 per year, is "perhaps the least busy official on the island.... Nobody bothers to read any more, one has only to press a button to listen to a professional give an excellent reading" ...for the books have been made into records. As for the newspapers and magazines, "they furnish only a momentary diversion for the mind, or even for the stomach. Yes! Some are actually printed on pastries in chocolate ink. Once read, one eats them at the next meal. Some are astringents, others have a slight purgative effect, and the body adjusts to them easily." [26]

The island has a tragic end when the rivalry between the Tankerdons and the Coverleys reaches such a peak that each clan takes over one of the two turbines, located on the port and starboard sides. The rivals refuse to coordinate the motors, and the torque created finally breaks up the metallic structure. Without misusing

[25] *Ibid.* p. 100.
[26] *Ibid.* pp. 97, 99.

clichés, is it not possible to say that Jules Verne makes capitalistic society perish as a result of its own inherent contradictions?

In the second part of Jules Verne's works, from 1890 onwards, the United States is no longer the privileged locus of scientific progress or the model for the future development of mankind, an experimental field for Verne's projections. In the novel of 1886, *The Clipper of the Clouds*, the engineer was the symbol of a society in the midst of expansion, full of confidence in the future of science. ("Robur *is* the science of the future," says Verne at the end of the novel.) But Robur reappears in another novel, *Master of the World*, published almost twenty years later, in 1904. (This is remarkable when we consider that the reappearance of characters is quite unusual in *Les Voyages extraordinaires*.) Robur is now an embittered misanthrope, at war with mankind, and hunted by the American police. Similarly, in *For the Flag* (1896), the United States tries to take over the military inventions of the scientist Thomas Roch, with the sole purpose of increasing its destructive, military potential. He is shut up in an insane asylum. Science has fallen into the hands of the military...

Jules Verne becomes more and more aware of the expansionist, imperialist nature of American politics. In *From the Earth to the Moon*, one of his first novels, where he is still enthusiastic about the United States as the privileged home of technical and industrial progress, he had already made note of the development of military science during the Civil War:

> Everyone knows how forcefully the military instinct developed in this nation of ship-owners, wholesale dealers, and merchants... The one preoccupation of this learned society [the Baltimore Gun Club] was the destruction of mankind for philanthropic ends and the perfection of arms, which were considered an instrument of civilization. It was a meeting of exterminating angels, who were nonetheless the best people in the world. [27]

---

[27] *De la terre à la lune*, pp. 1 and 4. It should be noted that the Indian Wars and the Indian resistance to American expansion, which played such

Jean Chesneaux

This tendency toward military strength and expansion is underscored more and more as Verne's image of the United States evolves. In *The Propeller Island,* the U.S. flag has 67 stars. "The American industrial and commercial power is at its peak after the annexation of the Dominion of Canada as far as the Arctic Ocean, the provinces of Mexico, Guatemala, Honduras, Nicaragua, and Costa Rica, up to the Panama Canal." [28] In *The Village in the Treetops,* the novel opens with discussion of a prospective American Congo: "the federal government will want its slice of the African pie some day," predicts one of the participants, more than half a century before the intervention of the U.N.'s "blue helmets" in the Congo at the instigation of the United States.

The satire of the American way of life, already biting in the *Propeller Island,* is pushed even farther in *The Day of an American Journalist in 2889.* This novelette was written in 1889 for an American magazine, *The Forum,* but the editors were not at all pleased by the sharp indictment it contained and demanded modifications. The full text was not published until after Verne's death, in the posthumous collection entitled *Yesterday and Tomorrow.* The United States, as Verne imagines it, has become inordinately powerful. It has annexed not only the whole New World, but also England, now its colony. The capital has been transferred from Washington to Centropolis; the *New York Herald* has become the *Earth Herald.* The mechanization of daily living has made immense progress, thanks to the use of electricity and waves of matter. It is possible to communicate across thousands of miles by "phonotelephoto," an instrument which permits people to see and talk with each other. A pneumatic tube puts Europe just two hundred ninety-five minutes away from the United States. Food is delivered to every home with no difficulty. Rural areas have lost all their rustic qualities and "are covered by a huge spider web of electric wires."

---

an important part in the development of American militarism, are not yet mentioned in *Les Voyages extraordinaires.* The Indians appear only in the guise of the Sioux marauders who attack Phileas Fogg's train (*Around the World in Eighty Days*). Jules Verne, like the good Saint-Simonian he was, doubtlessly felt the elimination of the Indians to be a "necessary evil."

[28] *L'Ile à Hélice,* p. 5.

On the other hand, "painting has fallen into such low estimation that Millet's *Angélus* has just been sold for fifteen francs, all because of the progress of color photography." All the while, advertising is bringing in three million dollars a day to the *Earth Herald,* "because of an ingenious system taken from a patent purchased for three dollars from a poor devil who died of starvation: it consists of huge posters, projected onto the clouds, the dimensions of which are so great that they can be seen in a whole country at once." [29] The main character of this fantastic story is Francis Bennett. A direct descendant of Gordon Bennett, founder of the *New York Herald,* he is one of the foremost men of the country. He owns huge factories like the central electric plant at Niagara. He lives in a palace of marble and gold. "The plenipotentiaries of every nation and the ministers themselves turn up on his doorstep, begging for his advice, seeking his approval, pleading for the support of his all-powerful organ. Just count all the scientists, artists, and inventors he supports." [30] And indeed, the reader is invited to listen in on the audiences he accords to foreign ambassadors, as well as to requests for subsidy that the scientists make of him. All this goes to show that Capital has become the master of politics and culture.

Francis Bennett laid the foundation of his power on a radical renovation of press techniques. He initiated "telephonic journalism." Each morning, instead of being printed, the *Earth Herald* is "spoken." It is in the course of a rapid conversation with a reporter, a politician, or a scientist that the subscribers learn what is of interest to them." [31] By these means, Bennett has raised the number of subscribers to eighty-five million, and his income to two hundred fifty million dollars a day, and his personal fortune to thirty billion dollars...

The image that Jules Verne formed of the United States — an image reflected in his novels — seems to be as complex and nuanced as

[29] *Hier et demain,* p. 188.
[30] *Ibid.* p. 180-181.
[31] *Ibid.* p. 180.

Jean Chesneaux

the American nineteenth century itself. From Franklin to McKinley, from Fenimore Cooper's pioneers to the gigantic fortunes of a Pierpont Morgan and a Hearst... In this image of the nineteenth century the profile of twentieth-century America is still quite indistinct. Jules Verne had been able to predict to some extent America's expansionism and technological alienation... But at his time, how was one to guess that this gigantic "megamachine" would be held in check by a small nation of modest, hardworking, determined, and unpolished people. The Vernian image is there to remind us that there was a time — somewhere in the past — when the hopes of forward-looking men and educators of youth tended to crystallize around a vision of the United States.

Translated by Frances Chew.

Jacqueline Flescher

The language of nonsense in *Alice*

Nonsense bears the stamp of paradox. The two terms of the paradox are order and disorder. Order is generally created by language, disorder by reference. But the essential factor is their peculiar interplay. Elizabeth Sewell, in a penetrating analysis of nonsense, stresses the idea of dialectic.[1] Yet her analysis deals almost exclusively with the formal structure of order. Emile Cammaerts, on the other hand, defines nonsense poetry as "poetry run wild."[2] This divergence clearly points to a danger: that of neglecting one dimension. An adequate definition must embrace both language and reference, order and disorder. The nature of their interaction must be underlined. Cross references and occasional repetition are therefore unavoidable. Moreover, the problem cannot be stated in simple terms. It is complex and elusive and constantly calls for qualification.

The first qualification concerns language. It is generally, though not necessarily, one of the forces at work. The backbone of nonsense must be a consciously regulated pattern. It can be the rhythmic structure of verse, the order of legal procedure, or the rules of the chess-game. Implicitly or explicitly, these three variations are all present in *Alice*. "Sentence first, verdict afterwards"[3] implies a knowledge of the normal sequence of events. Running backwards is a reversal of conventional order, legalized by the mirror; and the chess game provides a structural setting for inconsequential behavior. It is the

---

[1] Elizabeth Sewell, *The Field of Nonsense* (London, 1952), Chapter 5: "One and One and One and One and One".
[2] Emile Cammaerts, *The Poetry of Nonsense* (New York, 1926), p. 57.
[3] Lewis Carroll, *Alice in Wonderland* (*The Annotated Alice*, Forum Books: New York, 1963), p. 161. The following abbreviations will be used in subsequent quotations: AW: *Alice in Wonderland*. TLG: *Through the Looking Glass*. Both books will be referred to in the text as *Alice*.

Jacqueline Flescher

existent or implicit order which distinguishes nonsense from the absurd. It is the departure from this order which distinguishes nonsense from sense.

But language is constantly asked to provide the conscious framework. It is used more readily because it affords more possibilities of variation. The usual way of upsetting the conventional order of events is by reversal. This simple pattern is repeated constantly: "Hand it round first, cut it afterwards," (TLG, 290) "What sort of things do you remember best? ... O, things that happened the week after next." In this simple reversal, there is an implicit awareness of conventional order. If a character is simply caught up in a series of unconnected events which he cannot understand or control, or if he himself performs a series of actions of which one can determine neither the cause, purpose, nor inner relationship, we enter the realm of the Absurd: the hero of Kafka's *The Trial* is the victim of absurdity because he is trapped in a series of events which can be explained neither by their cause nor by their inner logic. So much for the distinction between nonsense and the absurd.

Language offers endless possibilities of upsetting the order of behavior, because it can establish a coherent system in a variety of ways. Provided that the backbone of such a system stand out clearly, it can act as a regulator for the most disorderly examples of behavior. The pattern of nonsense in this case is no longer one of simple reversal. It is a clash of opposing forces. The relationship between these two poles can best be described by an analogy: the content of nonsense is to its form what the content of poetry is to its metrical framework.

But rhyme and rhythm do not only provide an analogy. They are the very stuff of nonsense. An ordered system of language can by and large take two forms: inner relationship or serial progression (alphabet, declension, etc.). Metric pattern belongs to the latter category. In the following verse from *The Walrus and the Carpenter*, two elements contribute to a sharply defined order. These are rhythm and alliteration:

> The time has come, the walrus said,
> To talk of many things,
> Of shoes and ships and sealing-wax,
> Of cabbages and kings,
> And why the sea is boiling hot,
> And whether pigs have wings. (TLG, 235)

The metrical pattern stands out clearly because of its regular character. The alliteration in lines 3 and 4 reinforces the rhythmic pattern by accentuating the stressed syllables more heavily. Once the pattern has been so sharply defined, shoes, ships, and sealing-wax can co-exist happily, and cabbages and kings live side by side. Alliteration is widely used; assonance and internal rhyme are almost absent. The initial position of the stressed letter and the emphasis on consonants distinguish one rhythmic unit from another. Had Carroll exploited assonance, with emphasis on vowels, he would have weakened the function of the serial order.

It is the pattern provided by verse that makes verse a suitable vehicle for nonsense. But a similar pattern can also be attained, simply by exploiting a particular letter:

> ... and they drew all manner of things — everything that begins with an M.
> "Why with an M? said Alice.
> "Why not?" said the March Hare.
> — that begins with an M such as mouse-traps, and the moon, and memory, and muchness ... did you ever see such a thing as the drawing of a muchness? (AW, 103)

The letter M is chosen at random, but is subsequently repeated, and forms a pattern. Within this pattern, a free association of totally incompatible elements can be made: mouse-traps, the moon, memory, and muchness. Of course, this use of a simple letter assumes an autonomy of its own and eventually demands obedience from the author.

Jacqueline Flescher

The game "I love my love with an H" is based on a similar association:

> "I love my love with an H," Alice couldn't help beginning, "because he is Happy. I hate him with an H because he is Hideous. I fed him with Ham sandwiches and Hay. His name Haigha, and he lives..."
> "He lives on the Hill," the king remarked, without the least idea that he was joining in the game. (TLG, 279-80)

The process is exactly the same as in the previous example. The underlying principle of organization is the repetition of the letter H. It is the only link between "Happy, Hideous, Ham and Hay." Capitalization of the initial H's adds emphasis in the same way that alliteration reinforces the metric pattern. But the point of Carroll's formal arrangement is made clear in both the "M" and "H" examples by a final contrast. In the first case, the coined word "muchness" is isolated from its formal pattern in the question, "Did you ever see such a thing as the drawing of a muchness?" The effect, divorced from the repetitive pattern, is total absurdity. In the second case, the king unknowingly contributes to the formal pattern by joining in the game. The isolation from the formal context in the first example, the unconscious continuation of the formal context in the second, bring out by contrast the impact of the system.

Endless variations of this game can be found, ranging from the declension "A mouse — of a mouse — to a mouse — O mouse!" (AW, 41) to the rules of division and subtraction: "Divide a loaf by a knife — what's the answer to that?" "Take a bone from a dog: what remains?" (TLG, 321) The last two examples no longer show a serial relationship but an internal one.

The most complex example of a formal relationship in *Alice* is the Jabberwocky poem. Both the serial pattern of rhyme and rhythm and the internal grammatical structure are here combined. The poem does not easily lend itself to analysis. However, a juxtaposition of the first verse of the original and a recent parody of it might clarify peculiarities inherent in "Jabberwocky":

> *T'was* brillig *and* the slithy toves
> *Did* gyre *and* gimble *in* the wabe
> All mimsy *were* the borogroves
> *And* the mome raths outgrabe. (TLG, 191)

> *T'was* boodberg *and* the sliding tones
> *Did* hojer *and* haugen *in* the wade
> All semene *were* the homophones
> *And* emeneaus outgrade.[4]

The parody maintains all auxiliary verbs and conjunctions found in the original. The nouns, adjectives, and infinitives provide the variation. The author of the parody has simply kept the words indicating a relationship in the grammatical structure and varied the terms of the relationship. Humpty Dumpty's comment on words is revealing in this respect:

> They've a temper some of them — particularly verbs: they're the proudest — adjectives you can do anything with but not verbs..." (TLG, 269)

Humpty Dumpty, Lewis Carroll and the critics have attempted exact interpretations of the meaning of the words of "Jabberwocky." The variety of their conclusions perhaps indicates the futility of the enterprise. What critical analysis can stand the challenge of the following interpretation, which was made by a child: "It means a bug that comes out at night with a light on its tail and a sword between its beak. That's what a jabberwalkie is."[5] Another child gave a valu-

---

[4] By Professor Chao of The University of California, Berkeley. Read in the course of lecture on "Reversed Speech" given in the Linguistics Department of Yale, Spring 1969.
[5] Information provided by Miss Frances Calzetta, teacher of children's literature at Beecher Road School, Woodbridge, Connecticut.

Jacqueline Flescher

able key to the relationship between form and meaning: "He wrote it in language that almost makes sense when you read it. The words sound and are spelt like normal words in English, but the poem is imaginary in its physical language."[6]

Providing the sounds and the grammatical relationship survive, the sentence structure is not lost. It is, on the contrary, reinforced by the strong stress pattern and rhymes. Within this scheme, one can indulge in the wildest fancies without abandoning form. The portmanteau words are significant, not so much because of the specific meanings which they suggest, but because they embrace two disparate elements.

Meaning, however undefined, is nevertheless suggested. Preoccupation with meaning is constant throughout *Alice,* sometimes to an extreme degree. The whole range of relationships between word and reference, from total coincidence to exclusion of one of the two terms, can be found:

> "My name is Alice, but—"
> "It's a stupid name enough," Humpty Dumpty interrupted impatiently. "What does it mean?"
> "Must a name mean something?"
> "Of course it must." (TLG, 263)

Just as the obvious, matter-of-fact statement is common to the logic of the nonsense world, so the literal meaning is solicited where none exists:

> "Found *what*?" said the Duck.
> "Found *it*", the Mouse replied rather crossly. "Of course you know what it means." (AW, 47)

Whereas Humpty Dumpty tries to invest a name with meaning when none is implied, the duck looks for reference in a word that only

---

[6] Jonathan Lillian, age 12, Beecher Road School.

has grammatical function. Where figurative or functional meaning is intended, concrete significance is sought or understood. When the caterpillar asks Alice to explain herself, she shifts from the figurative to the literal meaning in her reply:

> "I can't explain myself, I'm afraid sir, because I'm not myself you see." (AW, 67)

Meaning is intensified so that language is always in the foreground.

Language can be emphasized, either by closing the gap between word and meaning and tightening the relationship, or, on the contrary, by widening the rift and weakening the relationship. In either case the balance between word and meaning is upset and the function of language becomes more apparent. Whenever Alice recites verses, she feels that the words "are coming different."

> ... her voice sounded hoarse and strange, and the words did not come as they used to do. ...
> ... "I'm sure those are not the right words," said poor Alice and her eyes filled with tears again as she went on. "I must be Mabel after all." (AW, 69)

The problem of personal identity is closely connected with the idea of estrangement from language. Alice's immediate conclusion on "not finding the right words" is that she can no longer be herself. This preoccupation with loss of identity is a recurrent one. But Alice views it with varying emotions. The complacent thought of sending her feet a pair of boots for Christmas is very different from the melancholy realization that she has just escaped from "shrinking away altogether." In the first case she humorously wards off her anxiety, in the second she is overcome by fear. This raises an interesting problem. At what point do we step outside the field of nonsense? The distinction between the two worlds is a finer one than critics have acknowledged.

Jacqueline Flescher

When Alice loses the objective control that enables her to view her problem of personal identity calmly, the mood becomes too disquieting to be "nonsensical." On using the word "juror," she feels proud of the extent of her vocabulary. The word "antipathies" is pronounced with misgivings. But both in her uneasiness and in her pride, Alice remains conscious of language and is able to control it; only when words betray her is the safety of her nonsense world threatened.

Insistence on speaking English is a safeguard against this threat:

> "Speak English," said the Eaglet. "I don't know the meaning of half those long words and what's more I don't believe you do either." (AW, 47)

Again and again, coherence and meaningful language are identified with the English tongue. French is resorted to when English is inadequate:

> "Perhaps it doesn't understand English," thought Alice. "I daresay it's a French mouse..." So she began again, "Où est ma chatte...." (AW, 41)

The queen advises Alice to "speak French" when she can't think of the English for a thing. (TLG, 212)

In "Looking Glass Insects," safeguards are removed and relationships between language and reference are completely broken down:

> "I suppose you don't want to lose your name?"
> "No indeed," Alice replied, a little anxiously. (TLG, 224)

When she reaches the wood where things have no name, her anxiety grows:

> "This must be the wood," she said thoughtfully to herself, "where things have no names. I wonder what will become of *my* name when I go in." (TLG, 225)

135

She unconsciously draws a parallel between the impossibility of naming things and the fear of losing her own identity:

> "I mean to get under the — under the — under the *this*, you know," putting her hand on the trunk of the tree. "What does it call itself, I wonder? I do believe it's got no name — why to be sure it hasn't!"
>
> She stood silent for a minute thinking: then she suddenly began again: "Then it really *has* happened, after all! And now *who* am I?" (TLG, 226)

In this moment of discovery, Alice feels the compelling power of things without a name. At the same time, she loses her hold on things. The exclusion of language immediately takes us beyond the playful level of argument. In her anguished monologue as in her compassionate relationship with the fawn, we are aware that she has become humanly vulnerable. Pride and self-control are forgotten. When she finally leaves the wood, she is relieved to have recovered her name, and hence her identity.

In "Tweedledum and Tweedledee," a reversed process may be observed. Things continue to have names, but the reality of the things rather than the names are questioned:

> "Well, it's no use your talking about waking him," said Tweedledum, "when you're only one of the things in his dream. You know very well you're not real."
>
> "I am real," said Alice, and she began to cry. (TLG, 239)

But the reality of Alice's tears is also questioned:

> "I hope you don't suppose those are real tears."

When either language or reference is threatened or destroyed, the playful argument of nonsense is abandoned. Alice no longer tries to

Jacqueline Flescher

"keep up her end" of the conversation. Her violent self-defense is an attempt to protect her identity.

So far, we have dealt essentially with the formal structure of nonsense. Clearly, the main concern is with relationship, whether it be serial or internal relationship between words, or the relationship between word and meaning. But nonsense is not simply a formal structure. Structure here runs counter to content. And content must be defined in its turn. We are immediately faced with a series of paradoxes. Order dominates the formal pattern, yet disorder seems to dominate reference. The characters are constantly preoccupied with meaning; yet their conversation is essentially meaningless. How can we account for this apparent contradiction?

To explain the divergence, we must once more go back to language. "When I use a word," says Humpty Dumpty, "it means just what I choose it to mean, neither more, nor less." (TLG, 269) When the king uses a word, he tests it out in an undertone: " 'important — unimportant — important —,' as if he were trying which word sounded best." (AW, 155) In both cases, the choice of meaning is arbitrary. Attributing a meaning to a word is an end in itself. "I'm sure I didn't mean," Alice says. "Well, you should have meant. What do you suppose is a child without meaning?" (TLG, 319) As shown previously, the weaker the link between word and meaning, the more nonsense is compromised. Total coincidence of word and reference is at the core of nonsense. Hence the frequency of the obvious fact and the literal meaning. Both arbitrary and obvious meaning are characterized by immanence, a kind of *en-soi* in the Sartrean sense. Meaning is often purely physical or factual. It leaves no room for speculation or suggestion and therefore refers to nothing beyond itself. It is in a sense self-contained. In spite of the necessity to *mean*, the power of meaning is reduced to a minimum.

The problem can be extended to conversation. Conversation, or more precisely, argument, is the essential vehicle of nonsense in *Alice,* but it is conversation of an unusual kind. It is based neither

The language of nonsense in *Alice*

on sustained discussion nor on coherent reasoning. The description of the caucus race immediately comes to mind:

> There was no "One, two, three and away!" but they began running when they liked, and left off when they liked, so that it was not easy to know when the race was over. (AW 48)

Many of the conversations and arguments in *Alice* are structurally reminiscent of this race.

What, in fact, determines the end of an argument in this context? Once more, it is a question of words. "The question is," says Humpty Dumpty, "which is to be master, that's all." (TLG, 269) Since the argument is not founded on logic, it leads nowhere. The sole aim of the characters involved is "having the last word." Within these arbitrary limits, how does the conversation develop? The principle is one of deflection. No argument is ever developed. It is immediately undercut, often by a misinterpretation. The word which is misinterpreted acts as a pivot and leads the conversation in a new direction. The pun is invaluable as a pivot for redirection:

> "Mine is a long sad tale," said the Mouse, turning to Alice and sighing. "It *is* a long tail certainly," said Alice, looking down with wonder at the Mouse's tail; "but why do you call it sad?" ... "I beg your pardon," said Alice very humbly, "you had got to the fifth bend, I think?" "I had *not*," cried the Mouse, sharply and very angrily. "A knot!" said Alice, always ready to make herself useful, and looking anxiously about her. "O do let me help to undo it." (AW, 52)

The two puns tale-tail, not-knot, provide a level of figurative meaning and another level of literal meaning. By taking the literal and not the intended meaning, the conversation is automatically channeled into a new direction. No sooner has it taken a new turn after the first pun, than a new pun sets it off in yet another direction. So the arguments are undercut before they can lead anywhere. Meaning remains at the surface; it can develop neither in depth nor in sequence. Unlike formal structure, which stresses relationship, referential structure destroys them. Random arguments proliferate on all sides, not as digressions diverging from a central meaning but as offshoots from language itself.

Puns are one way of deflecting meaning. Deliberate contradiction is another. Deliberate contradiction in *Alice* follows a recurrent pattern: a character will voice a basic refrain, with variations every time he is addressed:

> "*I've* seen gardens, compared with which this would be a wilderness."
> "When you say hill... *I* could show you hills, in comparison with which you'd call that a valley."
> "...You may call it nonsense if you like, but I've heard nonsense compared with which that would be as sensible as a dictionary." (TLG, 206-207)

Each new statement is met with a contradiction. The same basic refrain is used throughout: here, the modification simply consists of challenging a new word with its exact opposite. In "Looking Glass Insects," the chorus makes a brief comment after each stage of Alice's conversation with the guard. The comment is immediately followed up by the refrain, suitably modified to relate to the new situation:

> "Why his time is worth a thousand pounds a minute."
> "The land here is worth a thousand pounds an inch."
> "Why the smoke alone is worth a thousand pounds a puff."
> "Language is worth a thousand pounds a word." (TLG, 217)

The same process is used by the Duchess in "The Mock-Turtle's Story" when she finds a moral to match each one of Alice's statements.

The dogmatic finality of the contradiction or the refrain puts an end to the argument. Once more, development of ideas is evaded by deflection of meaning. The refrain emphasizes both the arbitrary character of the contradiction and the lack of progress in the conversation. Argument can either run in all directions or be repetitive. In either case, logical expansion of an idea is avoided: [7]

> "*You*, said the Caterpillar, "who are you?" which brought them back again to the beginning of the conversation. (AW, 67)

But absence of progression is concurrent with absence of depth. As coherent reasoning is cut short, so graver issues are kept at bay. Serious questions are interpreted as riddles and conversation is treated as a game:

> "However, this conversation is going on a little too fast: let's go back to the last remark but one"

says Humpty Dumpty. (TLG, 265) And in the same tone, the Red Queen suggests:

> "Make a remark, it's ridiculous to leave all the conversation to the pudding."

If conversation must remain superficial, arbitrary and literal, how is it integrated in the fantasy of Alice's wonderworld? Again, the answer seems to lie in paradox. Meaning is literal, but language is imaginative. It is language which governs meaning and determines the creative process:

> "Then you should say what you mean," the March Hare went on. "I do," Alice hastily replied, "at least I mean what I

---

[7] Another way of deflecting the meaning is by complicating thought and syntax to such an extent that we lose sight of the meaning: "Never imagine yourself not to be otherwise than it might appear to others that what you were or might have been was not otherwise than what you had been would have appeared to them to be otherwise."

Jacqueline Flescher

> say, that's the same thing you know." "Not the same thing a bit!" said the Hatter. (AW, 95)

The Hatter's objection is more significant than it appears. As we have noted, language in the nonsense world of *Alice* imposes a rigid order on the disorder of action and the incoherence of reasoning. This order is, however, essentially one of fixed relationships. Within the grammaical or metrical framework, vocabulary can be used with total freedom.

Puns, we noted, are a vital part of the creative process in *Alice*. But play on words can take different forms. The shift from figurative to literal meaning has a functional value. It redirects the conversation. The process of analogy and expansion sustains the conversation. It ensures the progression where rational meaning fails to do so:

> "... I only took the regular course."
> "What was that?" enquired Alice.
> "Reeling and Writing of course, to begin with," the Mock Turtle replied; and then the different branches of Arithmetic — Ambition, Distraction, Uglification and Derision." (AW, 129)

A whole area of experience is here transferred to a new context. Reality is undermined by the fantasy of the coined words. Yet it is implicitly alluded to in the analogy of sound. Here again, we touch on a crucial point. Reality remains implicit behind every manifestation of nonsense, but it is never explicitly represented. The nonsense world is a world of fantasy which shies clear of reality, yet indicates its existence.

The Mock-Turtle adds to his previous analogy:

> "The Drawling master: he taught us Drawling, Stretching, and Fainting in Coils"

and the Classical master taught "Laughing and Grief." (AW, 129-30) The whole passage on education has a metaphoric value. An organic unity is created with an imaginative interplay of vocabulary which refers back to a concrete area of experience. A variation on this technique is the process of analogy whereby one key-word is used with different compounds and grammatical functions:

> "You can draw water out of the water-well," said the Hatter, "so I should think you could draw treacle out of a treacle-well-eh, stupid?"
> "But they were in the well," Alice said to the Dormouse, not choosing to notice this last remark. "Of course they were," said the Dormouse: "well in." (AW 102)

The word "well" engenders a kind of proliferation. An imaginative progression is achieved through language; it is an example of language perpetuating itself. The same process accounts for the birth of the "snap-dragon-fly":

> "And there's a Dragon-fly."
> "Look on the branch above your head," said the Gnat, "and there you'll find a Snap-Dragon-fly. Its body is made of plum-pudding, its wings of holly leaves, and its head is a raisin burning in brandy."
> "And what does it live on?" Alice asked as before.
> "Frumenty and mince pie," the Gnat replied; "and it makes its nest in a Christmas box." (TLG, 223)

The initial image is built on a compound word: Snap-dragonfly. The coined word creates a new image composed of prosaic concrete elements which are woven into a thing of pure fantasy, set in the solid context of Christmas festivities. Prosaic reality and fantastic creation combine in this paradoxical creature of the nonsense world.

In nonsense, paradox is clearly found everywhere — in the relationships between language and meaning, order and disorder, formal pattern and imagination of language. But paradox must be qualified

Jacqueline Flescher

further. The relationships between the two terms of a paradox can be one of tension or of incongruity. Incongruity rather than tension prevails in the nonsense world. There is no conflict between language and reference. They follow divergent paths. We said earlier that the content of nonsense is to its form what the content of poetry is to its metric pattern. The analogy can be extended and qualified to bring out the distinction just made.

> I. An aged man is but a paltry thing,
> A tattered coat upon a stick, unless
> Soul clap its hands and sing, and louder sing
> For every tatter in its mortal dress.
> (W. B. Yeats, "Sailing to Byzantium")

> II. Prompt at the call, around the Goddess roll
> Broad hats, and hoods, and caps, a sable shoal:
> Thick and more thick the black blockade extends,
> A hundred head of Aristotle's friends.
> (A. Pope, "The Dunciad")

In these two examples the rhyming words are analogous in sound and divergent in grammatical function. The first shows a relationship of tension between the two rhyming words, the second of incongruity.

Incongruity brings us to the problem of humor. Is humor, as Elizabeth Sewell argues,[8] really incidental to nonsense? An absolute judgment cannot be made. But incongruity in *Alice* is certainly a key to its humor. Children's comments have been particularly revealing in this respect. A survey conducted among children aged ten to fourteen showed that a majority of children over thirteen found the *Alice* books both "unrealistic" and "stupid." The children who appreciated the fantasy also tended to appreciate the humor. A child of twelve made this apt distinction: "The words are silly but not stupid: they are ridiculous in a way that I like."[9]

---

[8] *The Field of Nonsense*, Chapter I.
[9] Jonathan Lillian, age 12.

Carroll's humor is of a particular kind. It is sheer, unadulterated fun, free from both topical allusion and from wit. It is intimately linked to the world of fantasy. Hence the kinship of nonsense with surrealism. The fetters of reality are broken and liberation is found in fantasy or laughter.

This blending of imagination and humor might well explain the fact that while isolated examples exist in France, nonsense has not become part of the literary tradition as in England. The greater propensity for whimsy of the English might well account for this difference in taste. With their emphasis on "esprit," the French tend to accept more reluctantly a gratuitous world that resists rational explanation.

Nonsense can be read at different levels. Like most great children's books, it is not simply a book for children. It can be read with the freshness of a child or the critical mind of an adult. Yet, in a way, a full appreciation of nonsense requires "a willing suspension of disbelief." The reader of the *Annotated Alice* has, in a sense, outgrown Wonderland.

Michael Holquist

What is a Boojum?
Nonsense and Modernism

> The other project was a scheme for entirely abolishing all words whatsoever; and this was urged as a great advantage in point of health as well as brevity. ... An expedient was therefore offered, that since words are only names for things, it would be more convenient for all men to carry about them such things as were necessary to express the particular business they are to discourse on.
> Swift, *Gulliver's Travels*

> What am I to do, what shall I do, what should I do, in my situation, how proceed? By aporia pure and simple? Or by affirmations and negations invalidated as uttered?
> Samuel Beckett, *The Unnamable*

Because the question "What is a Boojum," may appear strange or whimsical, I would like to begin by giving some reasons for posing it. Like many other readers, I have been intrigued and perplexed by a body of literature often called modern or post-modern, but which is probably most efficiently expressed in a list of authors: Joyce, Kafka, Beckett, Nabokov, Borges, Genet, Robbe-Grillet — the list could be extended, but these names will probably suffice to suggest, if very roughly, the tradition I have in mind. The works of these men are all very dissimilar to each other. However, they seem to have something in common when compared not to themselves as a class, but to past literature. In casting about for specific terms which might define this vaguely felt sense of what was distinctive and yet shared in these works, two things constantly inhibited any progress. The first was one's sense of the ridiculous: aware of other attempts to define the modern, one knew that it was difficult to do so without becoming shrill or unduly

What is a Boojum?

chileastic. There is a group of critics, of whom Ihab Hassan and Nathan Scott might be considered representative, who insist on an absolute cut-off between all of previous history and the modern experience. They have in their characteristically humorless way taken seriously Virginia Woolf's remark that "on or about December, 1910 human nature changed." The work of these critics is easily recognized in the apocalyptic rhetoric which distinguishes their writing, and in the irresponsible application they make of terms derived from modern German philosophy. Some rather thick books on the subject of recent literature could easily be reduced in size through the simple expedient of excising any mention of *Heimweh, Geworfenheit,* and that incantory word, *Angst.* So one thing which made it difficult to get at distinctive features in recent literature was the sense that it was very different from previous literature; and at the same time to recognize that it was not the end of history.

Another stumbling block, much less serious, was the constant recurrence of a phrase, which continually passed through my mind as I would read new works. I would read that Gregor Samsa woke up one morning to discover that he was an *Ungeziefer,* and immediately a ghostly refrain would be heard in my inner ear: "Aha, for the Snark *was* a Boojum, you see!" The same thing would happen when in *Lolita,* one discovered that all those strange men following Humbert were Quilty; or when reading in Gombrowicz that there was nothing to identity but the grimace [gęba]; and so on and on — one kept hearing "The Snark *was* a Boojum, you see." Pausing to reflect on this, the association of Lewis Carroll with modern literature seemed natural enough: his name figures in the first Surrealist manifesto (1924); Louis Aragon and André Breton write essays on Carroll; the former attempts a translation of *The Snark* (1929), the latter includes selections from Carroll in his *Anthologie de l'humour noir* (1939). Henri Parisot publishes a study of Carroll in 1952, in a series called, significantly, *Poètes d'aujourd'hui;* Antonin Artaud tried to translate the Jabberwocky song; Joyce's use of portmanteau words, without

Michael Holquist

which there would be no *Finnegans Wake,* is only one index of his high regard for Carroll; Borges admires Carroll, and Nabakov translates all of *Alice in Wonderland* into Russian (*Anja* v *strane chudes,* 1923). But such obvious associations of Carroll with modern authors were not, it turned out, the reason why the *Boojum* kept raising its head as I read these men.

Finally, I picked up again, after many years, *The Hunting of the Snark,* and it soon became apparent why its final line kept popping up in connection with modern literature: Lewis Carroll's "agony in eight fits" was not only among the first to exemplify what is perhaps the most distinctive feature of modern literature, it did so more openly, more paradigmatically than almost any other text one knew. That is, it best dramatized the attempt of an author to insure through the structure of his work that the work could be perceived only as what it was, and not some other thing; the attempt to create an immaculate fiction, a fiction that resists the attempts of readers, and especially those readers who write criticism, to turn it into an allegory, a system equatable with already existing systems in the non-fictive world. In what follows, I propose to outline this pattern of resistances in some detail as it exists in *The Hunting of the Snark,* and then, in a short conclusion to suggest the significance the pattern may have for readers of experimental modern fiction. But before looking at the poem itself, it might prove helpful to have some background information.

Lewis Carroll is, of course, a pseudonym. Characteristically for its bearer, it is an acrostic, based on an inversion of the re-Latinized forms of his two Christian names, Charles Lutwidge. Charles Lutwidge Dodgson is a fascinating object of study in himself, but in what follows I propose to mention only those aspects of his career which bear directly on the significance of the *Snark* poem.

Dodgson's whole career can best be understood as a quest for order, in some ways not unlike that of the White Knight in *Through the Looking Glass.* He begins his career as a student of mathematics, and was for many years a teacher of the subject in Christ Church College, Oxford. In his later years even the precision of Euclidian geometry failed to satisfy his lust for order, and he turned to symbolic logic. There are many anecdotes which further point up his compulsive orderliness: when he had packages to be wrapped, he drew diagrams so precise that they showed to a fraction of an inch just where the knots should be tied; he kept congeries of thermometers in his apartments and never let the temperature rise above or fall below a specific point. He worked out a system for betting on horses which eliminated disorderly chance. He wrote the director of Covent Garden telling him how to clear up the traffic jams which plagued the theater; to the post office on how to make its regulations more efficient. And after having written all these letters (more than 98,000 before he died), he then made an abstract of each, and entered it into a register with notes and cross references. When he saw the first proofs of *Alice in Wonderland,* he refused to accept them because, as his illustrator Tenniell had pointed out, they were not clear enough, a scruple which, however, did not keep him from selling the 2000 copies of this rejected printing to an American publisher, for whose colonial audience he felt the plates were adequate. When going over the plates for the illustrations to his last books, *Sylvie and Bruno* and *Sylvie and Bruno Concluded,* prepared by the artist Harry Furniss, Dodgson put them under a microscope in order to count the lines in the etchings. And then, in a gesture that is pure Nabokov, he compiled an index for these novels, complete with listings for "crocodiles, logic of" and "frog, young, how to amuse," all arranged from A ("Accelerated velocity, causes of") to W ("wilful waste, etc., lesson to be learnt from"). It should be clear that Dodgson's life, in the large outline of his whole career and in the smallest details of his everyday existence, was dominated by the quest for a more perfect order. I will return to the significance of this point in a moment. But one further aspect of Dodgson/Carroll's existence should first be mentioned. It concerns the necessity of the slash or hyphen which one must use when referring to this author. That is, he is both Charles Lutwidge Dodgson, student (or Fellow) of Christ Church, and Lewis Carroll, author of books of nonsense.

Michael Holquist

Queen Victoria herself became aware of the split when, having been delighted in 1865 by *Alice in Wonderland,* she asked that a standing order be left for the author's next book; in 1866 she was not amused when she was given Dodgson's formidably technical *Condensation of Determinants.* Another revealing story is told by one of the child friends from Dodgson's later years, Isa Bowman, who grew up to write a book about her benefactor. As a young girl he took her to see one of those static panoramas so beloved by the Victorians. It was a diorama of Niagara Falls, with the figure of a dog in the foreground. Dodgson amused her by spinning a tale in which the dog was really alive, but trained to stand motionless for hours on end. He "...added other absurd details about the dog, how, if we waited long enough, we should see an attendant bring him a bone, how he was allowed so many hours off each day when his brother, who unfortunately was rather restless, would take his place, and how this badly behaved animal on one occasion jumped right out of the panorama among the onlookers, attracted by the sight of a little girl's sandwich, and so on. Suddenly he began to stammer and looking round in some alarm, I saw that a dozen grown-ups and children had gathered around and were listening with every appearance of amused interest. And it was not Mr. Carroll but a very confused Mr. Dodgson who took me by the hand and led me quickly from the scene." [1] Much has been made of this dichotomy between Mr. Carroll and Mr. Dodgson, and psychoanalytical studies, such as Phyllis Greenacre's *Swift and Carroll* (New York, 1955), suggest that the man was simply a schizophrenic who found a unique means of adjustment.

A more balanced view has been provided in what are probably the two best studies of Carroll: Elizabeth Sewell's *The Field of Nonsense* (London, 1952) and Alfred Liede's *Dichtung als Spiel* (Berlin, 1963, 2 vols.). These two critics have suggested that the split between Dodgson and Carroll is only an apparent dichotomy, quickly resolved if one sees that there is a common pursuit at the heart of each avatar, a *Drang nach Ordnung* which Dodgson/Carroll sought in mathematics and logic, in the strictly ordered life of an Oxford

---

[1] Cited in R. L. Green, *Lewis Carroll* (New York, 1962), p. 25.

scholar, in the severely proper existence of a Victorian gentleman—and last but not least, in nonsense. In fact it was in nonsense that Dodgson's compulsion toward order found its most perfect expression, a point that has also been made by a professor of logic at Leeds University, Peter Alexander. [2] I would further add that the most nonsensical nonsense which Carroll created is *The Hunting of the Snark*. There is an ascending progression toward the apex it represents in 1876, from the first Alice book (1865) through the second (1872); and all the work after the *Snark* was a decline, a falling away which is painful in the last books, *Sylvie and Bruno* (1889) and *Sylvie and Bruno Concluded* (1893).

The *Snark* is the most perfect nonsense which Carroll created in that it best exemplifies what all his career and all his books sought to do: achieve pure order. For nonsense, in the writings of Lewis Carroll, at any rate, does not mean gibberish; it is not chaos, but the opposite of chaos. It is a closed field of language in which the meaning of any single unit is dependent on its relationship to the system of the other constituents. Nonsense is "a collection of words of events which in their arrangement do not fit into some recognized system," [3] but which constitute a new system of their own. As has recently been said, "what we have learned from Saussure is that, taken singly, signs do not signify anything, and that each one of them does not so much express a meaning as mark a divergence of meaning between itself and other signs... The prior whole which Saussure is talking about cannot be the explicit and articulated whole of a complete language as it is recorded in grammars and dictionaries... the unity he is talking about is a unity of coexistence, like that of the sections of an arch which shoulder one another. In a unified whole of this kind, the learned parts of a language have an immediate value as a whole, and progress is made less by addition and juxtaposition than by the internal articulation of a function which in its own way is already complete." [4] My argument here is that *The Hunting of the Snark* constitutes such a

---

[2] *Logic and the Humor of Lewis Carroll* (Leeds, 1951).
[3] Sewell, p. 25.
[4] Maurice Merleau-Ponty, "Indirect Language and the Voices of Silence," *Signs*, tr. Richard C. McCleary (Northwestern U. Press, 1964) pp. 39-40.

whole; it is its own system of signs which gain their meaning by constantly dramatizing their differences from signs in other systems. The poem is, in a small way, its own language. This is difficult to grasp because its elements are bound up so closely with the syntax, morphology, and, fleetingly, the semantics of the English language.

Some illustrations, taken from Carroll, may help us here. In the book which most closely approximates the completeness of the system in the *Snark, Through the Looking Glass,* Humpty Dumpty says in a famous passage: " 'When *I* use a word... it means just what I choose it to mean—neither more nor less.' 'The question is,' said Alice, 'whether you *can* make words mean so many different things.' 'The question is' said Humpty Dumpty, 'which is to be master—that's all.' " This last remark is a rebuke to Alice, who has not understood the problem: it is not, as she says, to "make words mean so many *different* things." It is to make a word mean just *one* thing, the thing which its user intends and nothing else. Which is to be master—the system of language which says " 'glory' doesn't mean 'a nice knockdown argument' " or Humpty who says it does mean that, and in his system, only that. Nonsense is a system in which, at its purest, words mean only one thing, and they get that meaning through divergence from the system of the nonsense itself, as well as through divergence from an existing language system. This raises, of course, the question of how one understands nonsense. It is a point to which I will return later; for the moment suffice it to say that if meaning in nonsense is dependent on the field it constructs, then the difference between nonsense and gibberish is that nonsense is a system which can be learned, as languages are learned. Thus the elements of the system can be perceived relationally, and therefore meaningfully, within it. Gibberish, on the other hand, is unsystematic.

What this suggests is that nonsense, among other things, is highly abstract. It is very much like the pure relations which obtain in mathematics, where ten remains ten, whether ten apples, ten horses, ten men, or ten Bandersnarks. This is an important point, and helps to define one relationship of nonsense to modernism. For it suggests a crucial difference between nonsense and the absurd. The absurd points to a discrepancy between purely human values and purely logical values. When a computer announces that the best cure for brain cancer is to amputate the patient's head, it is, according its system, being logical.[5] But such a conclusion is unsettling to the patient and absurd to less involved observers. The absurd is a contrast between systems of human belief, which may lack all logic, and the extremes of a logic unfettered by human disorder. Thus the absurd is basically play with order and disorder. Nonsense is play with order only. It achieves its effects not from contrasting order and confusion, but rather by contrasting one system of order against another system of order, each of which is logical in itself, but which cannot find a place in the other. This distinction may help to account for the two dominant modes of depersonalization in recent literature. The absurd operates in the theater, where the contrast of human/non-human serves to exploit the presence of living actors on the stage. Nonsense, understood as defined above, dominates in prose fictions, where the book may become its own hermetic world, its own laboratory for systematic play, without the anthropomorphizing presence of actors. Thus the difference between, say, Beckett's *Waiting for Godot,* and the same author's *Comment c'est*.

Lewis Carroll is one of the most important figures in the movement Ortega y Gasset has called the "dehumanization of art." Kafka was not the first to reduce his hero to an integer; his K has an earlier analogue in one of the many essays Dodgson wrote on Oxford university issues. In 1865 the Regius chair in Greek fell vacant, and Dodgson used the occasion as an inspiration for a little paper called *A New Method of Evaluation of* π: "Let U=the university, G=Greek, and P=professor. Then GP=Greek Professor; let this be reduced to its lowest terms and call the result I. Also let W=the work done, T=the times, p=giving payment, π=the payment according to T, and S=the sum required; so that π=S. The problem is to obtain a value for π which shall be commensurate with W..."

---

[5] For raising the problems of the relationship between nonsense and the absurd, and for the computer example, I am grateful to my friend Jan Kott.

Michael Holquist

"Let this be reduced to its lowest terms..." What Dodgson has expressed here in satire is a fundamental principle of his nonsense. For to reduce a word to one meaning is surely to reduce language to its lowest terms. The effect is to create a condition of what the Russian critic Viktor Shklovsky has called *ostranenie,* or "making it strange." But, again like so much modern literature, the effect in the *Snark* is not just to estrange a character or an event, but to estrange language itself. The technique is usually employed to render some familiar action unfamiliar by describing it naïvely, as if perceived for the first time. And this is what nonsense does to language. But it has a purpose for doing so, one which Merleau-Ponty has hinted at in another context: "If we want to understand language as an originating operation, we must pretend never to have spoken, submit language to a reduction without which it would once more escape us by referring us to what it signifies for us, [we must] *look* at [language] as deaf people look at those who are speaking." [6] Or, it should be added, *look* at language as children or Lewis Carroll *look* at language.

In order to understand "language as an originating operation" we must, in other words, see it as a process, as a system in itself. By so doing, one becomes aware of its capacity to present us with something new. But in order to achieve this state of radical linguistic innocence it is necessary to put aside all expectations which arise from the habit of creating meaning through systems other than language. Perception has recently been defined as being "primarily the modification of an anticipation." [7] The unfamiliar is always understood in terms of the familiar. [8] This may seem a bit opaque, but it is really quite simple, and an operation we engage in and see performed every day around us. The most common example of it in literary criticism is found in the work of critics who bring to bear on any given text a procrustean system, the sort of thing T.S. Eliot had in mind when he referred to the "lemon-squeezer school" of criticism. A rigidly

---

[6] Merleau-Ponty, *Ibid,* p. 46.
[7] J. R. Beloff, "Perpection and Extrapolation," *Bulletin of the British Psychological Society,* XXXII (May 1957), 44.
[8] See E. H. Gombrich, *Art and Illusion* (Princeton U. Press, 1960), pp. 63-92.

Freudian critic will never perceive a dark, wet setting as anything but a womb symbol, or an object which is slender and vertical as anything but a phallic symbol, regardless of the fact that, in the system of the text he is treating, the former is a bower in a forest, say, or the latter a cane or spear. This critic has not seen bowers or spears in the one system because his expectations are a function of another system. In order to see a new thing we must be able to recognize it as such, and this is done by the willed inhibition of systems we have learnt before coming upon the novel object, an act performed in the service of learning new systems. If this is not done in literary criticism, all texts become allegories. The *Odyssey* ceases to be an epic system with properties peculiar to it alone, and becomes an Allegory of Quest; *Gulliver's Travels* ceases to be a satiric structure with its own distinctive features, and is turned into an allegory of Swift's psychological development, an orgy of Freudian Anality; Dostoevsky's novels become equally orgiastic allegories of Sin and Redemption.

Critics of Lewis Carroll have possibly developed this allegorical urge to its ultimate limits. Phyllis Greenacre, a practicing psychiatrist, cannot forget that Dodgson loved to photograph little girls in the nude, with results for her interpretation of the Alice books which are as predictable as they are unfortunate. [9] Louis Aragon, in a 1931 article in *Le Surréalisme au service de la révolution* does a Marxian interpretation of the Alice books, notable for such insights as: "in those shameful days of massacre in Ireland... human liberty lay wholly in the frail hands of Alice..." William Empson has combined Freudian and Marxian techniques in his reading, "The Child as Swain." [10] Alice experiences birth trauma, and her tears become amniotic fluid; commenting on the famous scene at the end of *Through the Looking Glass* where Alice pulls off the tablecloth, sending plates, dishes, and guests hurtling to the floor, Empson remarks, "It is the High Table of Christ Church we must think of here..." [11] A. L. Taylor makes the Alice

---

[9] Greenacre, *op. cit.*
[10] *Some Versions of Pastoral* (London, 1935).
[11] *Ibid.*, p. 294.

books into that easiest to find of all allegories, the Christian.[12] I have argued that the Alice books are less perfect nonsense than *The Hunting of the Snark*; therefore they are less hermetic, less systematic in their own right, and thus more porous to other systems.

But even the *Snark* has not excaped the allegorist. Alexander Taylor sees it as an anti-vivisectionist tract [13] and Martin Gardner, in his otherwise fine annotated version, suggests a crude existentialist reading, full of *Angst's,* and in which the Boojum somehow becomes the atomic bomb.[14] A former dean of the Harvard Business School has argued that the poem is "a satire on business in general, the Boojum a symbol of a business slump, and the whole thing a tragedy about the business cycle."[15] I will not go into F. C. S. Schiller's theory, which states that the *Snark* is a satire on Hegelian philosophy, because Schiller presents his theory as a send-up. But even W. H. Auden has said that the *Snark* is a "pure example" of the way in which, "if thought of as isolated in the midst of the ocean, a ship can stand for mankind and human society moving through time and struggling with its destiny."[16]

Now there is something remarkably wrong about all this. Dodgson himself would be astounded. We have his word that "I can guarantee that the books have no religious teaching whatever in them— in fact they do not teach anything at all."[17] It may be that, knowing how drearily and relentlessly didactic Victorian children's books were, readers have not been able to accept that the most famous representative of the class is without uplift of one sort or another. However a quick comparison of *Alice* or the *Snark* with Charles Kingsley's *The Water Babies* (1863) should be enough to convince any unprejudiced reader of the fact. Kingsley's book, it will be remembered, ends with Tom, the erstwhile fairy, "now a great man of science [who] can plan railroads and steam engines, and electric telegraphs and rifled guns,

---

[12] *The White Knight* (Edinburgh, 1952).
[13] Taylor, *op. cit.*
[14] Martin Gardner, *The Annotated Snark* (New York, 1962), p. 25.
[15] *Ibid.*, p. 19.
[16] *The Enchafèd Flood* (New York: Vintage Books, 1967), p. 63.
[17] Letter cited in Roger Lanclyn Green, *Lewis Carroll* (New York, 1962), p. 52.

What is a Boojum?

and so forth." Not content with this, the author adds, to his little readers in the attached "Moral," "...do you learn your lessons, and thank God that you have plenty of cold water to wash in; and wash in it, too, like a true Englishman."

Lewis Carroll does not cloy in this way because he had a very sophisticated image of his audience. One may be highly specific about what the word child meant to Charles Lutwidge Dodgson. It meant first of all a girl; further, a girl between the ages of ten and thirteen, who belonged to an upper-middle class family; was beautiful; intelligent; well dressed and well behaved. Anything else was not a child. Now it is obvious that such a restricted view of children cannot be the same one which animates Lewis Carroll the author. Rather, this audience is conceived not in terms of chronology, but as a state of perceptual innocence and honesty. Children are the proper audience of nonsense only to the degree that they let strange things remain strange; to the degree they resist forcing old systems on new, and insist on differences rather than similarities. The allegorists who have written about the *Snark* without having *seen* it are obviously long past such a state of open potentiality.

The best argument against the *Snark*'s allegorization remains, of course, the poem itself. The interpretation which follows is based not only on the poem itself, but on the various ways in which it *is* itself. That is, the poem is best understood as a structure of resistances to other structures of meaning which might be brought to it. The meaning of the poem consists in the several strategies which hedge it off as itself, which insure its hermetic nature against the hermeneutic impulse. Below are six of the many ways by which the poem gains coherence through inherence.

1. The dedication poem to Gertrude Chataway appears at first glance to be simply another of those treacly Victorian set pieces Dodgson would compose when he abandoned nonsense for what he sometimes thought was serious literature. But a second reading reveals that the poem contains an acrostic: the first letter of each line spells out Gertrude Chataway; a third reading will show that the initial

word in the first line of each of the four quatrains constitute another acrostic, Girt, Rude, Chat, Away. This is the first indication in the poem that the words in it exist less for what they denote in the system of English than they do for the system Carroll will erect. That is, the initial four words of each stanza are there less to indicate the four meanings present in them before they were deployed by Carroll they at first convey (clothed, wild, speak, begone) than they are to articulate a purely idiosyncratic pattern of Carroll's own devising.

2. Another index of the systematic arbitrariness of the poem is found in the second quatrain of the first Fit: "Just the place for a Snark! I have said it twice: / That alone should encourage the crew. / Just the place for a Snark! I have said it thrice: / What I tell you three times is true." The rule of three operates in two ways. First of all it is a system for determining a truth that is absolutely unique to this poem. When in Fit 5 the Butcher wishes to prove that the scream he has heard belongs to a Jubjub bird, he succeeds in doing so by repeating three times, "Tis the voice of the Jubjub!" Now, there will be those who say that there is no such thing as a Jubjub bird. But in fact, in the system of the Snark poem, there is—and his existence is definitively confirmed through the proof which that system *itself* provides in the rule of 3. In the game of nonsense that rule, and only that rule, works. The system itself provides the assurance that only it can give meaning to itself.

The rule of three also operates as a marker, indicating that the intrinsic logic of the poem is *not* that of extrinsic logic which operates in systems outside the construct of the poem. In other words, it is a parody of the three components of that core element in traditional logic, the syllogism. As an example of this, take an exercise from Dodgson's own book, *Symbolic Logic* (1896): "No one has read the letter but John; No one, who has *not* read it, knows what it is about." The answer is, or course, "No one but *John* knows what the letter is about." The third repetition "Tis the voice of the Jubjub," has the same effect in nonsense that the third part of the syllogistic progression has in logic. The *Oxford Universal Dictionary* defines a syllogism as a major and a minor premise, "with a third proposition called the conclusion, *resulting necessarily from the other two*." If you begin with nonsense, and its conclusion, like the syllogism, results necessarily from the beginning, you also end with nonsense. The progression is closed to other systems. It is not, incidentally, without significance for Carroll's play with words that the etymology of syllogism is a portmanteau from the Greek *syllogizesthai* (to reckon together) and *logizesthai* (to reason) which has its root, *logos*.

3. The same effect of an arbitrariness whose sense can be gleaned only from the poem itself is to be found in the various names of the crew members: Bellman, Boots, Bonnet-maker, Barrister, Broker, Billiard-marker, Banker, Beaver, Baker, and Butcher. They all begin with a B. And much ink has been spilled in trying to explain (from the point of view of the allegory a given critic has tried to read into the *Snark*) why this should be so. The obvious answer, if one resists the impulse to substitute something else for the text, is that they all begin with B *because they all begin with B*. The fact that they all have the same initial sound is a parallel that draws attention to itself because it is a parallel. But it is only a parallel at the level where all the crew members on this voyage will be referred to by nouns which have an initial voiced bilabial plosive. In other words, it is a parallel that is rigidly observed, which dramatizes itself, but only as a dynamic *process* of parallelism, and nothing else.

4. Another way in which the poem sets up resistances which frustrate allegory is to be found in the fifth Fit. The butcher sets out to prove that two can be added to one. "Taking three as the subject to reason about — / A convenient number to state — / We add seven and ten, and then multiply out / By one thousand diminished by eight.

The result we proceed to divide, as you see, / By nine hundred and ninety and two: / Then subtract seventeen, and the answer must be / Exactly and perfectly true."

Michael Holquist

And in fact the answer is perfectly true — but it is also what you begin with. The equation begins with 3 — the number the Butcher is trying to establish — and it ends with 3. The math of the equation looks like this: $\dfrac{(X+7+10)(1000-8)}{992} - 17 = X$; which simplifies to x, or a pure integer. The equation is a process which begins with no content and ends with no content. It is a pure process which has no end other than itself. It is thus perhaps the best paradigm of the process of the whole poem: it does what it is about. It is pure surface, but as Oscar Wilde once observed, "there is nothing more profound than surface."

5. A fifth way in which the poem maintains its structural integrity is found in the many coinages it contains, words which Humpty Dumpty defines as portmanteau words, two meanings packed into one word like a portmanteau; words which Giles Deleuze, in the most comprehensive study of Carroll's significance for language, *Logique du Sens,* has so charmingly translated as "les mots-valises." [18] Carroll, in the introduction to the *Snark* writes, "...take the two words 'fuming' and 'furious.' Make up your mind that you will say both words, but have it unsettled which you will say first. Now open your mouth and speak. If your thoughts incline ever so little towards 'fuming' you will say 'fuming-furious;' if they turn by even a hair's breadth towards 'furious,' you will say 'furious-fuming;' but if you have that rarest of gifts, a perfectly balanced mind, you will say 'frumious.' "

"If you have that rarest of gifts, a balanced mind...," in other words, you will find just the right word, and not some approximation. In the seventh Fit, when the Banker is attacked by the Bandersnatch, the bird is described as having "frumious jaws." And the Banker, utterly shaken, chants "in mimsiest tones," a combination of miserable and flimsy. For a bird which exists only in the system of nonsense, adjectives used to describe objects in other systems will not do; they are not precise enough, and so the system itself provides its own

---

[18] Paris: Editions de Minuit, 1969, p. 59; see also pp. 268-78.

adjective for its own substantive. Since only the Banker has ever been attacked by a Bandersnatch, it is necessary to find a unique adjective adequate to this unique experience: thus "mimsiest." This attempt to find just the right word, and no other, resulting finally in coinages, is another way in which Carroll's search for precision, order, relates him to language as an innovative process in modern literature. Carroll speaks of "that rarest of gifts, a balanced mind" as the source of his experiment. In our own century it was a man remarkable for *not* possessing that gift who has best expressed the pathos of its absence in the face of language. In one of his fragments Antonin Artaud says "there's no correlation for me between *words* and the exact states of my being... I'm the man who's best felt the astounding disorder of his language in its relation to his thought." [19] Carroll's portmanteau words are revealing not only for the way they participate in the self-insuring autonomy of the poem. They also provide an illustration of how Carroll's nonsense is grounded in a logic of surface. The portmanteau word is not only a combination of two definitions, it is a combination of two systems, language and logic. Mention was made earlier of Saussure's insight into the way language *means* through *divergence*. The portmanteau word creates a new meaning by phonologically exploiting the divergence between two old meanings. It thus provides one of the most economical proofs of Saussure's insight into language. But the portmanteau word is also the third element of a three-part progression, from one, furious, to two, fuming, to three, frumious. Like the rule of three it results in a new "truth," and like the rule of three it is a unique kind of syllogism. In order to get a logical conclusion to the syllogism, it must grow out of a divergence between two prior parallel statements.

This is an important point if one is to see the logic which determines that Carroll's system is a *language* and not gibberish. In logic, not all pairs of apparent concrete propositions can result in a meaningful conclusion. Two examples, again taken from our poet's own textbook of *Symbolic Logic* will make the point. The two statements, "No riddles interest me if they can be solved"; and "All *these* riddles

---

[19] *Artaud Anthology*, ed. Jack Hirschman (San Francisco, 1965), p. 37.

are insoluable," cannot lead to a conclusion due to the fallacy of like eliminads not asserted to exist. "Some of these shops are not crowded; no crowded shops are comfortable" cannot lead to a conclusion due to the fallacy of *un*like eliminads with an entity-premise. These and other possibilities for false syllogisms are generally subsumed under the fallacy of "post hoc, ergo propter hoc." That is, the invalidity of the conclusion is a result of incorrect premises. And the criterion for determining whether the primary and secondary propositions are *valid* or not is provided by the rules of logic itself. These rules make up one system. But if one were to create *another* system, which would state that the original premises were correct according to *its* rules, then the same conclusion which the system of logic would call invalid would, perceived as a result obtained according to the new rules, be correct. By extrapolation a true syllogism has been created out of what was in another set false.

The point this arcane diversion into eliminads and entity-premises seeks to make is that the system of Carroll's nonsense is just such an extrapolation, it is the transcendence of the post hoc, ergo propter hoc principle into an aesthetic. Carroll's portmanteaux are *words* and not gibberish because they operate according to the rule which says that all coinages in the poem will grow out of the collapse of two known words into a new one. Carroll can deploy words he invents and still communicate, because he does so according to rules. Whereas an expression of gibberish would be a sound pattern whose meaning could not be gleaned from its *use* according to rules: an expression of gibberish would be a sound pattern whose meaning could not be gleaned either from the syntactic or morphological principles provided by its use, or which would be deducible according to such principles in a known language system. Nonsense, like gibberish, is a violence practiced on semantics. But since it is systematic, the sense of nonsense can be learned. And that is the value of it: it calls attention to language. Carroll's nonsense keeps us honest; through the process of disorientation and learning which reading him entails, we are made aware again that language is not something we know, but something alive, in process — something to be discovered.

6. The final structure of resistance I'd like to mention is contained in perhaps the most obvious feature of the poem, its rhyme. William K. Wimsatt, in a well-known essay, makes the point that in a poem the rhyme imposes "upon the logical pattern of expressed argument a kind of fixative counterpattern of alogical implication." [20] He goes on to say that "rhyme is commonly recognized as a binder in verse structure. But where there is need for binding there must be some difference or separation between the things to be bound. If they are already close together, it is supererogatory to emphasize this by the maneuver of rhyme. So we may say that the greater the difference in meaning between rhyme words the more marked and the more appropriate will be the binding effect." This important insight into verse is contained in a piece entitled "One Relation of Rhyme to Reason." Now, Lewis Carroll wrote a book entitled *Rhyme? and Reason?* (1883), and I suggest that the distinctive role which rhyme plays in the *Snark* is best caught by means of a titular portmanteau here. That is, it is precisely that one relation of rhyme to reason which Professor Wimsatt evokes in *his* title, which is put into question marks not only by *Carroll's* title of 1883, but which is also put into question in the function rhyme serves in *The Hunting of the Snark*.

Professor Wimsatt suggests that "the words of a rhyme, with their curious harmony of sound and distinction of sense, are an amalgam of the sensory and the logical, or an arrest and precipitation of the logical in sensory form; they are the icon in which the idea is caught." [21] I read this to mean that two words which are disparate in meaning result, when bound by rhyme, in a new meaning which was not contained in either of them alone. In other words, you get a kind of rule of three at work. Like the syllogism, two disparate but related elements originate a third. Thus understood, the rhyme of traditional verse has the effect of meaningful surprise;

---

[20] *The Verbal Icon* (New York, 3rd Noonday edition, 1962), p. 153.
[21] *Op. cit.*, p. 165.

two rhymes will constitute a syllogism resulting in a new association.[22]

But this is not true of nonsense verse. "They sought it with thimbles, they sought it with care;/ They pursued it with forks and hope;/ They threatened its life with a railway-share;/ They charmed it with smiles and soap." This stanza begins each of the last four Fits, and may stand as an example for what rhyme does throughout the poem. The rhyme words, "care, railway-share," and "hope, soap" would be very different from each other in traditional verse, and binding effects of the sort Professor Wimsatt has demonstrated in Pope or Byron would be possible. Because the language of most verse is simply a more efficiently organized means of making sense of the sort that language *outside* verse provides. Thus, while very different, some kind of meaningful association could be made of them capable of catching an idea.

But "care," "railway share," "hope" and "soap" in this quatrain have as their ambiance *not* the semantic field of the English language, but the field of Carroll's nonsense. In traditional verse "rhyme words ... can scarcely appear in a context without showing some difference of meaning."[23] But if the whole context of a poem is *without* meaning, its separate parts will also lack it. There can be no differences in meaning between words because they are all equally meaningless in this context. So the reader who attempts to relate rhyme to meaning in Carroll's poem will be frustrated. The syllogism of rhyme, which in other verse has a new meaning as its conclusion, ends, in Carroll's verse, where it began. Instead of aiding meaning, it is another strategy to defeat it. Language in nonsense is thus a seamless garment, a pure cover, absolute surface.

But if *The Hunting of the Snark* is an absolute metaphor, if it means only itself, why read it? There are several answers, but the one I have chosen to give here is that it may help us to understand other, more complex attempts to do the same thing in modern literature. It is easy to laugh at the various casuistries by which

---

[22] For a detailed study of sound/sense patterns in verse see: A. Kibedi Varga, *Les Constantes du poème* (The Hague, 1963), pp. 39-42, 91-121.
[23] Wimsatt, p. 156.

readers have sought to make an allegory, something else, out of the *Snark*. But the same sort of thing is being done every day to Kafka or Nabokov. Possibly the example of Lewis Carroll may suggest how far we must go, how much we must forget, how much we must learn in order to see fiction as fiction.

For the moral of the *Snark* is that it has no moral. It is a fiction, a thing which does not seek to be "real" or "true." The nineteenth-century was a great age of system building and myth makers. We are the heirs of Marx and Freud, and many other prophets as well, all of whom seek to explain *everything,* to make sense out of *everything* in terms of one system or another. In the homogenized world which resulted, it could be seen that art was nothing more than another — and not necessarily privileged — way for economic or psychological forces to express themselves. As Robbe-Grillet says, "Cultural fringes (bits of psychology, ethics, metaphysics, etc.) are all the time being attached to things and making them seem less strange, more comprehensible, more reassuring." [24]

Aware of this danger, authors have fought back, experimenting with new ways to insure the inviolability of their own systems, to invite abrasion, insist on strangeness, create fictions. Lewis Carroll is in some small degree a forerunner of this saving effort. To see his nonsense as a logic is thus far from being an exercise in bloodless formalism. That logic insures the fictionality of his art, and as human beings we need fictions. As is so often the case, Nietzsche said it best: "we have art in order not to die of the truth."

After having stressed at such length that everything in the *Snark* means what it means according to its own system, it is no doubt unneccessary, but in conclusion I would like to answer the question with which we began. What is a Boojum? A Boojum is a Boojum.

---

[24] "A Path for the Future of the Novel," in Maurice Nadeau, *The French Novel Since the War,* tr. A. M. Sheridan Smith (London, 1967), p. 185.

Richard Howard

Childhood amnesia

for Laurent de Brunhoff

The French do not have children. Or childhood. What they have, as all of us know who have accepted Baudelaire's invitation, is infants. And infancy. Not childsplay — *enfantillage*. The French have sons and daughters, the schools are full of boys and girls, but there are no *children*. In other words, in *one* other word, the French have what their language has foisted upon them, for every culture has the vocabulary it reserves: they have *relations*.

Enfant. From the Latin *infans*; from *in* (not) and *fari* (to speak): the one who does not speak.
Fable. From the Latin *fabula* (narrative, story), from *fari* (to speak).

Put them together and it spells ... silence. Secrecy — perhaps the only secret ever kept in France. The Gentlemen's Agreement, the *tacit* complicity of the French concerning childhood is as absolute and reliable as the understanding of two of Sade's characters concerning the use of the garrotte or the presence of the mother. As in most Mediterranean cultures, there is no French word for *child*, no word for the human young taken, or given, not as a relation, not as an element in a structure, but as a reality, a self, a center, a surd.

> It is noticeable that writers who concern themselves with explaining the characteristics and reactions of the adult have devoted much more attention to the primeval period comprised in the life of the individual's ancestors — have, that

> is, ascribed much more influence to heredity — than to the other primeval period which falls within the lifetime of the individual himself — that is, to childhood. —Freud (1905).

Of course there are evasions, disclaimers, disguises, colloquial proxies. The French employ — invent, invoke, indulge — their celebrated *argot* (a "secret jargon," as of thieves; the word's origin is unknown) whenever they seek to conceal, to distract attention from, what they are doing. That is why they have the richest slang in the world.

Yet it is only an expedient, their argot, a cover-up: it must be reinvented every generation or so, for it sinks into the sand of experience and is lost, like the origin of the word *argot* itself. *Gosse* is a stopgap, a makeshift, a *circumlocution* which is a way of talking around... a secret. What matters is what is done with the language in its central range, not around the edges — what matters is not Francis Carco but Jean Genet:

> My first impulse was to point out to him that it was ridiculous to put words and phrases between quotation marks, for that prevents them from entering the language. When I received his letters, his quotation marks made me shudder — a shudder of shame. Those quotation marks were the flaw... whereby my friend showed that he was himself, and that he was wounded. —*Miracle of the Rose* (1951).

And in the central range of the French language, there is no word for *child*; no childishness in that closed circuit, that strict discourse which is the entire justice of French Literature. A literature of relations, in which all are *members,* marvellously combined, subordinated, distributed: a continuum.

It was Gide, with his splendidly personal sense of Vicissitude, of diverging, opposing, and ultimately complementary... ultimates

Richard Howard

("*les extrêmes me touchent*"), who perfectly characterized French Literature (which he could not escape any better than could Genet or Sade, the world's freest minds in the world's most imprisoned bodies) as one immense and endless conversation. And if to eavesdroppers like ourselves it sounds more like an argument than a *causerie,* that is merely because we have not been listening long enough. For the dialogue continues, the unappeasable do-it-yourself dialectic proceeds, asking questions not to be answered for five hundred years, answering others the season before they are asked — a system of provocation and response without a temporal variable:

> Hydre absolue, ivre de ta chair bleue,
> Qui te remords l'étincelante queue
> Dans un tumulte au silence pareil.

At any given point of entry, the reader of this Literature has the encircling, often constricting awareness — has the *conviction* — that he is inside a completed structure, as the foreign visitor to Paris frequently has the suspicion, crossing even the broadest steppes the city affords — the Place de la Concorde under a stormy sky, the Jardin du Luxembourg on a sunny afternoon — that all of Paris is really *inside,* somehow preposterously enclosed and housed in one enormous chamber, and a *salon* at that!

The pride of it all, and the horror, is that it keeps going on, apparently able to assimilate whatever is proposed, even whatever is opposed (as Gide opposed to it the Bible, Shakespeare, Dostoievsky, even Dashiell Hammett), a myth of our human happening. Endless this sense of stylization; the only unpunished French vice and certainly the only unpublicized one, such accommodation may operate either upward or downward, as F. W. Dupee once pointed out — we may get something like *Steinbeck-ou-les-nobles-sauvages,* or we may get *Hamlet-ou-le-distrait.* And if the great solitaries of modern British and American literature are still unknown in France, it is because the French have not yet found the right stylistic frame for Hardy and Yeats, for Stevens and Frost. *Ça viendra.*

French Literature, like Sainte-Beuve, is "inclined to accumulate incompatibles" — whereat they are found to lie down together, like Villon and Genet, like Bossuet and Péguy, who harmonize with each other more closely than with analogous figures outside the fold. Recuperative, burrowing, exorbitantly metropolitan, in this voice is the resonance of an entire human survival, the interminable, unnameable gossip in which Mr. Beckett, of course, has the last word — last, because it is also the first:

> I'll go on, you must say words, as long as there are any, until they find me, until they say me, strange pain, strange sin, you must go on, perhaps it is done already, perhaps they have said me already, perhaps they have carried me to the threshold of my story, before the door that opens on my story, that would surprise me, if it opens, it will be I, it will be the silence, where I am, I don't know, I'll never know, in the silence you don't know, you must go on, I can't go on. —*The Unnameable* (1949).

A literature of childhood? The words have not found it, no word has uttered it. Not yet. For the child — momentarily: how long is childhood? — is not a member, is not accommodated, is not an infant, an *enfant*. The child *has* his word to say, has to say *his* word, a word that carries him to the threshold of his story, before the door that opens on his story, and it will be a word unknown — for how long? — to French Literature. Precisely: as Mr. Beckett is at such pains to reveal, speech begins only in the face of the unnameable, upon the perception of an *elsewhere* alien to the very language which seeks it out. It is this creative doubt of the child, this fecund aporia of his language which French Literature, until very recently, has condemned to silence in its "central range" and exorcized around the edges.

If there have been children in French Literature, they are there as mere instances of acculturation; as victims (Hugo, Renard), as cult objects (Hugo again, Gide); either assimilated by Society as in-

Richard Howard

fants (speechless) or transformed into members (remembered) or extruded as freaks (Minou Drouet). Until yesterday, the child as an acceptable (utterable) metaphor of human life had no place, no word, in France.

When we think of what Shakespeare and Goethe, Blake and Dostoievsky invented — remembering that to invent is to find, *invenire* to come upon — we may be startled that *l'Opoponax* is the first book — however trivial, however complacent — of its kind in French, the first to acknowledge *another language*.

But we will understand why there has been no children's literature in France.

Contributors

PHILIPPE ARIES, author of *L'Enfant et la vie familiale sous l'ancien régime* (known in English as *Centuries of Childhood*) is currently at work on a study of changing social attitudes toward death. MARC SORIANO teaches at Bordeaux; his recently-published book, *Les Contes de Perrault: culture savante et traditions populaires*, won the Prix Sainte-Beuve. MARTHE ROBERT is a psychoanalyst who has written extensively on literature; her publications include *L'Ancien et le nouveau, de Don Quichotte à Kafka*, a translation of Kafka's correspondence, and the volume of essays, *Sur le papier*. Educator, editor and critic of children's books, ISABELLE JAN is presently writing a major history of children's literature.

ESTHER S. KANIPE is a graduate student in history at the University of Wisconsin, specializing in nineteenth-century French intellectual history, and preparing a thesis on attitudes toward children in the works published by Hetzel. MARION DURAND is a nursery school teacher and critic of books for children. Of the Yale French Department is ANDRÉ WINANDY. The professional speciality of JEAN CHESNEAUX is Southeast Asian history, which he teaches at the University of Paris; Jules Verne is an avocation to which he has devoted several articles. JACQUELINE FLESCHER taught in the Yale French Department for three years, and has now returned to France to take a position at the Sorbonne. Yale Slavicist MICHAEL HOLQUIST is currently on leave in Leningrad. Poet, critic, translator, RICHARD HOWARD has most recently published a study of contemporary American poets, *Alone With America*, and will soon bring forth a third volume of poetry.

LAURENT DE BRUNHOFF has continued and expanded into many realms the celebrated *Babar* series begun by his father. PETER BROOKS, of the Yale French Department, recently published *The Novel of Worldliness*, a study of eighteenth-century French fiction.